Down the Wild Rivers

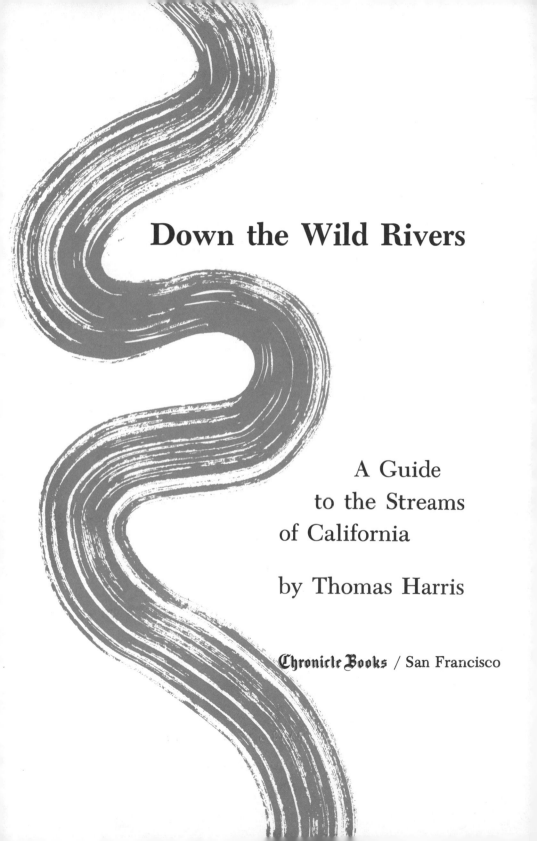

Down the Wild Rivers

A Guide
to the Streams
of California

by Thomas Harris

Chronicle Books / San Francisco

To my son Vance—a true voyageur.

Contents

Foreword

LONG before there were endless ribbons of concrete stretching over every horizon, California's wild rivers were its only highways. The soft swish of a paddle, the sure eye of a riverman, and the throbbing currents provided swift and silent passage throughout the state. Small bands of Indians coasted along these waters, their crude dugouts filled with wild berries and fresh venison. Trappers descended the endless watery staircases to get their furs down to market. Explorers traversed the rivers to map the trackless wilderness through which they flowed.

But gradually the land became more crowded and hurried. There was no longer time for the river passage, for floating along constantly at the whim of sudden surging rapids or long placid stretches of flat water. Highways and cities fanned out in every direction, suffocating forever the beautiful and fertile wilderness beneath.

Ironically, now that we need to escape this urban madness and cleanse our minds and souls, our billion-dollar freeway system can't take us back into the remaining wild country of California. Forgotten for nearly a century, and battling to survive the mindless abuses we have heaped upon them, the rivers are now the only paths back into the wilderness. Canoeing, kayaking, or rafting down the rivers offers that last sweet chance to escape the week-long suburban madness and savor the inspiring aroma of dew-freshened meadow grass, fragrant conifers, and a wholesome morning meal sizzling over a campfire. The rivers also offer one of the final avenues of escape from the maddening crowds that swarm to the "wilderness" beaches, campgrounds, and mountain retreats of the state.

These pages are dedicated to those who have felt the growing frustration of seeing their favorite campsite over-run by the summertime transistor crowd, and to those who have despaired of the opportunities for their children to know the land as it used to be. This book was written to reforge a link with a past too long ignored, to rekindle the spark of adventure, to refresh long-discarded memories of the wildly musical song of a lonely loon, the brilliance of the Milky Way framed by a dark and towering forest, the thrill of the river's surging, cascading bid for freedom as it races seaward, the soft, peaceful gurgle of a mountain river meandering peacefully through verdant, silent glades.

The following pages serve as the only volume we know of to provide a written guide to the better recreation-boating rivers of a state richly endowed with glorious waterways. The more suited to the modest abilities of the casual family boaters, the more definitively the rivers are described. The Klamath, Trinity and Eel rivers, for instance, are described almost from their head-waters to their mouths because they represent such a priceless possession. As the last of the state's wild rivers and because they must be ranked among the finest canoeing waters in the nation, they are grouped together first. Following in succession are the wonderful assortment of rivers coursing down the western slopes of the Sierra Nevada, then the rivers mainly of the Sacramento Valley, and, finally, the coastal streams.

A note of caution: No matter how detailed the scouting descriptions get, nor how intensely you read them, the author neither wants nor expects blind obedience. Coursing down a rapid doesn't permit much time for jotting notes about the absolutely precise location of each potential hazard. Even if it did, winter storms change a river's path slightly from year to year, pushing a key boulder a few yards this way or that. Don't expect this book to do your guiding for you.

Caution and respect make ideal mixers with river water. Arrogance or carelessness, on the other hand, can leave a most sour taste in the mouth. Keep your eyes open, your mind alert, and you will find yourself in harmony with the magical song of the rivers. But, be in too much of a hurry or too cock-sure to scout or pause for a closer look, and that gurgling ally below can turn into a surging, angry foe intent upon giving you a lesson you may never forget—or one you may never get another chance to remember.

Without any apologies, there are some rivers not mentioned in these pages and others talked of only fleetingly. Space was reserved for what the author considers the best boating waters for average weekend boaters. There are many more challenging waterways waiting to be explored, and you may be lucky enough to experience the exhilaration and pride of discovering a new run and passing on the good news to others.

In a time when the words "river" and "environment" conjure only thoughts of pollution and man's arrogant tampering with nature, it is reassuring to know that the wild back country is still there, just out of sight and earshot of the neon lights, the blaring jukeboxes, and the boggling crowds. And to reach this country, you need only abandon the roads and highways and take to the water—*Down The Wild Rivers*.

The Escape

Our Escape
to the Wilderness

WE stood quietly on the shore of the Russian River, watching
eddies swirl where the current cascaded into the trunk of a giant
oak sheared off by the winter floods. The sturdy aluminum tips
of our rented Gruman canoes jutted out from the shore on a
long rocky bar just beneath Alexander Valley Bridge, about 10
miles, by road, north of Healdsburg. Apparently, I had not been
able to mask the apprehension that I was beginning to feel as
I studied the river and the cross-rip where the main current
slammed into the bridge abutment and churned itself into a short,
swift chute. My wife Glenda said what I had been thinking:
"Are you sure we can make it?"

We knew the rudiments of canoeing, having paddled around
the summer before in the pristine beauty of Waterton Lake,
in the Canadian Rockies. But river touring was something new.
And although the Russian River was reputed to be an excellent
beginner's course, the power of the currents was somewhat un-
settling. I helped Glenda and our youngest daughter Lynette
into the slim craft. Our teenagers Vance and Valorie were standing by with their own canoe. I gave them the high sign, and
we all shoved off into the middle of a deep pool.

At first, our boat slid forward effortlessly, with only a light
swishing as the bow sliced through the water. Then there was
a rocking motion and a light moan as the shell of the boat scraped
against a dripping snag. We were free again almost instantly
and made a good recovery, but our faces must have betrayed
the mild panic we had felt. The kids in the glide below were
laughing uproariously at our momentary plight.

Each stretch of rapids brought more delightfully errant maneuvers. On those we misjudged, we usually wound up temporarily
tangled in the underbrush. "I'm not so sure about this," laughed
Glenda more than once as she knifed the bow paddle into the

water, sculling to bring us out of a snarl. It was a delicious and preposterous morning.

In but a few hours, appetites were sharpened by the exercise, and the pleasant coolness of the water beckoned enticingly. Our front-running and tireless teenagers finally swerved into a sheltered pool ahead and motioned for us to follow them onto a narrow spit of coarse river sand. Two turtles, the size of small frying pans, had been sunning when our not-so-silent approach interrupted their siesta and sent them with a splash into the river. Giant oak, cottonwood, and dogwood trees and a lower level of drooping willows formed a canopy overhead that shut out all but the most persistent rays of the noonday sun. It was not entirely unlike a jungle scene. Graceful streamers of moss trailed from the limbs of the oaks. Turkey vultures soared silently in the thermal updrafts above and saucy blackbirds sent up a steady and somewhat raucous chorus from the willows. It suddenly occurred to me that those noisy blackbirds and soaring vultures and skittish turtles were at home here and that we five city slickers had at last found a small patch of wilderness.

We beached the canoes, stretched out some grass mats beneath a shady oak, and then swam and sunned ourselves before eating lunch. Finally, I lay in the warm sun, devouring a leg of chicken and slowly thinking back over the past few months. What had put us here on this river—a newspaperman, his wife, and their three children, people who had become more at home on a freeway? A year ago, even this quiet river would have looked impressive and impassable to us. What were we doing canoeing along a twisting California river, greenhorns so far out of our element?

We had slowly grown more and more frustrated and hemmed in by the insanity of megalopolism. And we had grown weary and disappointed with the usual summer trip—a quick dash into the mountains or to the coast, always fighting the hordes of other frustrated city dwellers trying to catch even a brief glimpse of what was left of nature. But no matter how we had tried to stay to the out-of-the-way places, the "Sorry: Campground Full" and "By Reservation Only" signs preceded us in every campground and state park. We had just been born 100 years too late, it seemed.

But it was more than the inviting freedom of a quiet sand

Canoeing is a full family undertaking for author's
brood, right down to "Tiger," the adventuresome
poodle. Vance, his mother Glenda, and sisters
Lynette (front) and Valorie select tryout craft from
rental fleet on the Russian River for first float trip
on one of the state's classic canoe rivers.

bar or shaded pool that we were seeking on this river outing. The helter-skelter life in suburbia was slowly driving a wedge into the heart of our family. Eighteen years of marriage, with good times and bad, welds links between man and wife that survive such strains. But the connections to teenagers are much more fragile and demanding.

Vance's struggle with adolescence was, alternately, a painful, puzzling, pleasing, and maddening thing. Valorie, at 14, was just beginning to show the swells of womanhood, and the mother-daughter relationship was undergoing increasing strain. Even Lynette, at 6, was able to turn things upside down with comparative ease and exasperating regularity. We knew the older ones would always stretch for a bit more freedom and independence than we were either willing or anxious to give; the wing-flapping was not unexpected. But the intensity of the practice flights was oftentimes unexpected and even alarming.

The signs had become obvious. The family malady was suburban withdrawals, at least the beginning stages of them. We had seen the terrible price that other families had paid for that social infection, spread by a virus of drugs, parental neglect, and a life style growing more hectic, environmentally abusive, and artificial by the day. It was powerfully evident that our future as a close-knit family was at stake in this, our experiment along the Russian River.

It was Glenda who first suggested that a canoe run might be our best chance for the "something special" that we both knew our family needed. She was right. The blissful peace of a smooth, swift glide through the clear water, with primeval vistas of trees and banks flashing silently by on either side, seems to rekindle the soul. We all felt that same surge of freedom. The odds for our future seemed a bit shorter now, the frayed family ties a bit sturdier.

I sat up to reassure myself that we really had rented two canoes and taken on this adventure on the Russian River and that I wasn't just dreaming about a more promising future for the family. Our picnic lunch was long since past and the water was reoccupied quietly by three pinking bodies. Lynette was paddling around the shallows in her life jacket, chasing tadpoles and minnows. Vance and Val were floating aimlessly, like bits of driftwood caught in an eddy.

"It's even better than we planned, isn't it?" Glenda's voice was low and warm. I turned to look at her and found that she, too, was reveling in the delight and contentment of her brood. Later, as we alternately drifted through the small but exciting chutes ahead and paddled along the slower stretches nearing Del Rio Woods Dam, it became abundantly clear that this was indeed much better than we had planned or hoped.

The ride home to Fremont, along San Francisco Bay's eastern shore, was an excited babble of plans for greater and greater conquests. We knew where we would be spending our next summer vacation and our autumn holidays and a good deal of the time beforehand. We were through with dusty, noisy campgrounds. From now on, we would be found along some verdant and peaceful river, thrashing about in its pools or dashing down its occasional mane of white foamy rapids.

During the next few months, we honed our paddling skills on other stretches of the Russian River and on the swifter American River, above Sacramento, where it rolls through the lower foothills of the Sierra. Our outfitting for these trips was gradual and keyed to practical and discovered needs. A 15-foot Starcraft aluminum canoe became the mother ship to a flamboyant two-man inflatable kayak. The latter craft was not quite as swift or maneuverable as the canoe; but it was more than its equal in buoyancy, and it was easily transportable. We added lightweight sleeping bags that could roll up small, some basic camping utensils and dehydrated food, and we were fully prepared for a more ambitious expedition. Then, after weeks of map reading and a score of telephone calls to members of various river-touring sections of the two Sierra Club chapters in the Bay Area, we pinpointed the ideal site for our forthcoming summer adventure. We would make a five-day run through the majestic wilderness of the Trinity and Klamath River canyons in the far northern reaches of the state.

During our drive northward, we paused in the heartland of the majestic redwood groves along U.S. 101. Glenda and I had previously sampled the reverence and kinship with Mother Earth and her Creator that those stately groves impart. And now, we were watching it pulse through our offspring as they craned their necks skyward to drink in the magnificence of those forest kings. A moment of family prayer in that glistening cathedral was the most natural thing in the world and a fine way to begin our soul-building adventure.

A few hours later, we were sweating out the broiling heat of the August sun in the Trinity National Forest. We had turned off the highway at Salyer Forestry Station, crossed the Trinity on a high and rickety wooden bridge, and, looking for a place to launch, headed upriver on a narrow, paved, frontage road. Three miles further on, as we left the pitted pavement and bounced down a steep gravel road, we saw the river curl into a quiet backwater. A turnout took us down to a little clearing beneath a scattering of pine and dogwood. We parked the car there and started the unloading.

For more than an hour in the 95-degree heat, we stumbled up and down the sandy path to the river, carting the boats and the six GI-style rubberized laundry bags that encased our supplies. Then, as the rest of the tribe lashed down the gear, I drove the car back to Salyer for safekeeping and caught a ride back, perched somewhat precariously on the back of an obliging young man's small motorbike.

On my return, I found that the chaos at riverside had given way to a certain level of organized confusion. We nosed out into the current and were soon gliding swiftly downstream. The Trinity is a raging torrent in winter flood, but on this midsummer day, its water was gin-clear and warmed by a heatwave to a record 76 degrees.

A stretch of rapids suddenly sprang out of nowhere. The spray broke over the gunwhales and splashed both Glenda in the bow seat and Lynette beside the bedrolls in the middle. The swiftness of the current and the solid "thunk-thump" as the canoe bounced over the chop was exhilarating. Were it not for the roar of white water, our loud whoops of delight would have been heard for miles.

As it was, our progress was virtually silent; and darting around a bend in the river, we startled a group of rather intimately preoccupied sunbathers. Their mid-day amorous activities may have been well-screened from the highway a quarter of a mile above, but they were unguarded from our unsuspected vantage point. Heels and shapely buttocks scooted off in every direction.

A mile or two further on, deep in the heavily forested canyon, the river had gouged out a deep pool from the solid rock wall

State parks may be full during busy summer
season, but isolated banks of the Trinity River near
Willow Creek offer perfect shoreline camp sites.
Placid pools like this make the Trinity one of the
best canoe camping rivers in the state.

that flanked it. The emerald hue of the pool beckoned us from the current, and we paused there for a cooling dip in the crystal clear water. The kids dove for silver coins, easily visible 12 feet down among the smooth rocks on the bottom.

Refreshed and ready for more challenges, we headed downstream again toward Willow Creek, still at least 12 river miles away. Our tiny regatta, enraptured and slightly anxious captives of the current, snaked along the isolated canyon floor, hurtling over one set of rapids after another. Hawks spiralled slowly, effortlessly overhead, riding the thermal swells. Saucy bluejays flew back and forth between the canyon walls and chattered from the pine boughs, scolding the invaders. The canyon was a carpet of green, and I could envision the breathtaking blaze of color that would sweep the area in two more months—the brilliant scarlet of maple leaves and the bright yellow of flowering dogwood gilded by the first nights of frost. Then, the predominant deep green of the Douglas fir would serve only to accentuate the fall finery of the canyon walls.

An hour or so later, only 8 miles into our planned 15-mile first-day run, we pulled into camp on a sandy bluff. We beached our boats high up on a rock-strewn bar so they would not be swept away should the river level rise in an unannounced release from the dam at Lewiston, about 50 miles upriver. Later, content with a warm and filling supper and snuggled in our bags, we watched the red eyes of the fading coals and relived the excitement, hazards, and scenic glories of the day's run. The night sounds began to stir, punctuating our laughter and story-telling. I lay back and looked upward. The years of smog and city lights had dulled my memories of the brilliance of this star-lit universe, but it all came vividly back to life in a glittering endless sky that made eternity seem more believable.

The others dropped off to sleep quickly, peacefully. I remained awake, listening to the pulsating river sounds—the soft gurgle of the long smooth glide just below camp; the dull, almost imperceptible throb that signaled a rapids not far beyond. This was the unmistakable sound of freedom; the wild, pure water dashing downward to the sea, pausing where the topography allowed or demanded it but never ceasing, never tamed. The civil engineers have a more prosaic name for such natural occurrences: "uncontrolled rivers." Whatever they are called, such river scenes, with their incredible beauty and serenity, are more and more precious as they have become more and more scarce in California.

I pondered, as I sat staring into the blinking coals of the campfire, what the future held for the wild rivers of California, especially the three remaining great rivers, the Trinity, the Klamath, and the Eel. Was the state merely stalling for time when it promised a thorough reevaluation and at least a 10-year delay in its mammoth and controversial water project? Would it, in 10 years, still try to enslave the wild rivers forever, to harness their pulsing currents to hydroelectric plants or to divert their lifestream into an endless concrete spawning channel for the relentless metropolitan glut in the Southland beyond the Tehachapis?

It's one thing to know a river at a distance, as would the motorists stealing a quick sidelong glance or the angler venturing into a modest riffle for a longer cast. But it's quite another thing to go beyond that casual acquaintance to the intimate, vibrant relationship that has fired the blood of rivermen since the days of the crude dugouts. It is intoxicating and unique, this experience of feeling a river's every thrust and surge for freedom as it whisks you through plunging chutes and over frothing rapids in a canoe, kayak, or raft. And there is a special, indefinable eloquence about a silent glide over mirrored river pools in the depths of a perfect primeval wilderness. The subtle, yet detectable difference between tamed and untamed rivers is soul-building in its own quiet way: a natural waterline etched by small pockets of moss and pebbles polished shiny by the steady throb of current as compared to the telltale streaks of greyish white left on the rocky banks by the constant fluctuation of the water level.

There was no conscious thought of it, but a silent prayer began welling up within me. Let these wondrous artistries of the Creator be left alone. No more ugly scars. No more man-made abuses. Leave these surviving rivers to run free and majestically to the sea from what is left of their once-pristine headwaters.

Suddenly, my thoughts were interrupted. I had been slumped drowsily on my sleeping bag, head propped against an old snag and eyes skyward, drinking in the brilliance of the stars as they sparkled to life above the faint rim of the canyon. Now an outburst of clattering rocks brought me bolt upright, heart pounding, as I looked out into the night. I scanned the shore quickly and there, bounding majestically out of the water and over the rocks, was a huge buck. His six-point rack soared in soft outline against a faint moonlight glow and glistened with wetness from his midnight swim across the narrows below camp. It's one thing to know a river at a distance; it's quite another to become an organic part of its gentle magic.

The succeeding two days on the Trinity were a mixture of lighthearted frolicking in peaceful riverside pools and a few serious hours as we learned to guide our crafts through swift stretches of swirling rapids. We continued confidently toward Weitchpec and the confluence where the swifter, more dangerous Klamath tumbles powerfully toward the Pacific. Enroute, there were short pauses as we plucked handfuls of luscious ripe blackberries from a drooping bush in Hoopa Valley, spent another magical night at riverside in the isolated Trinity Gorge, and negotiated two fairly easy portages around throbbing rapids.

The water of the Klamath turned out to be much swifter than our scouting reports had indicated. In addition, the currents criss-crossed dangerously, lacing the stream with sucking undertows. Still, we maneuvered for a full day through a dozen churning, frothy stretches of the Klamath's white water, suffering nothing more serious than a good soaking from the spray that broke over the gunwhales as we sliced through the boiling spouts of the rapids. When we had passed the heat of mid-day and the shadows were beginning to stretch out from the tree-shrouded shore, hunger pangs sounded quitting time for our first day on the Klamath. A long gravel bar on the left tapered off into a willow thicket. We pulled in there, beached the boats on the fine sand, and sent the kids scouting for a campsite.

They soon found a sheltered clearing in the sand, behind some high rocks and almost surrounded by the willows. It was a choice under-the-stars campsite. Lynette was assigned to the firewood detail and came back from the shore dragging a tree branch that dwarfed her. "I didn't even have to chop it down," she announced proudly. That she didn't have an axe in the first place was completely beside the point; she knew that we preferred to live with Mother Nature, not off of her.

Great blue herons, their raucous cries echoing between the canyon walls, awoke us the next morning at sun-up. And with the savory aroma of pancakes and fried Canadian bacon, the herons were soon joined by a mixed gallery of chattering fearless bluejays and a big bushy-tailed squirrel. We finished breakfast

High bluffs of the upper gorge of the Trinity, just
below Willow Creek, provide scenic backdrop to
this pair of river paddlers as they cruise by modest
tributary on one of the state's finest pieces of Class
I-II water.

and while the girls cleaned up, Vance and I repacked the supply
bags, lugged the gear down to the boats, inflated the kayak, and
lashed the gear into the canoe. Then we were off again, the
Starcraft leading the way downstream to a take-out point I had
selected the night before.

The moment we pushed off from shore on this last lap of our
journey to the ocean, I felt for the first time a real twinge of
unease. We were about 5 miles upstream from the Orleans bridge
and the water looked very rough. We found out later that while
some parties have completed the challenging Klamath run from
below Ishi Pishi Falls (upstream from Orleans) to the ocean, there
are also some on record whose attempts have ended in disaster,
either during high water or because of carelessness or inexperi-
ence. Others simply had to give up the struggle, including our
presumptuous little regatta, which was to be pummeled and sent

packing by the wild rapids entrapped in the deep box canyon half a day's run below Orleans.

However, before we were engulfed and defeated in that dangerous canyon passage, we enjoyed one moment of breathtaking triumph. As expected, the take-out point I had selected turned out to be just above a thunderous drop, where the river funnels into a narrow surging rapids. We pulled over to shore to assess the stretch ahead, and even from that distance the dancing manes of the white horses in midstream looked ominous. A portage would have meant unpacking and repacking all of the gear—nearly an hour of labor—and, yet, this water looked well beyond our ability and experience. Still, there was one thin slick down its seething midsection that seemed to offer comparatively safe passage, so after a long look and detailed consultation on shore, Vance and Val walked back upstream and climbed into their bobbing kayak. They would try it.

They stroked in unison, powering the boat out into the racing current. Then dancing and bobbing on the frosted water like a fallen leaf, the kayak swept into the slick V at the mouth of the main funnel. White water thundered all around the kids and the kayak as they shot the rapids, sliding broadside for a panic-stricken moment up the crest of the most treacherous spout and then straightening out in the swift chop below.

Getting the deeper hulled canoe through that stretch seemed more dangerous, but there was no easy alternative. Lynette and Glenda walked along the bank, Val waited downstream, and Vance and I cautiously paddled the canoe out into the current. It was like a roller-coaster ride—bucking, darting, and wildly exciting. Some powerful sculling strokes curved us around a cluster of angry rocks and we were finally gliding through the chop in the pool below. The girls rejoined us and Vance returned to the kayak; then we headed into what our observations and scouting reports described as about 2 miles of quiet glides in which the river took a breather in its wild dash to the Pacific. Vance and I were still flushed with excitement, our nerve ends tingling. No narcotic could give you a high like that.

Stroking only occasionally at the stern to maintain direction, we drifted peacefully downriver. For the first time on the run, the safer, lighter kayak was not leading the way; we assumed that there was nothing to fear. The ominous roar of fast water had always signaled the approach of danger in plenty of time for us to find a pull-out for a safe and sensibly cautious look at what was ahead. It was nearing mid-day and the temperature was soaring into the 90s again. Foolishly, we allowed Lynette to take off her lifejacket.

Then, without a murmur of advance notice, a deep, angry, gurgling sound brought me bolt upright, desperately scanning ahead for its source. What I saw turned my innards icy. Instinctively, I knew there was no time for evasion. The river was running at almost a record low level that summer, exposing for the first time in 20 or 30 years a sharp 4-foot drop about 4 miles south of Orleans. The scouting reports hadn't mentioned the drop, of course; it had never been there during higher water.

Four feet might not be much as waterfalls go, but for an open canoe, fully loaded, it spelled disaster. The boat shot over the edge and dropped sickeningly into the broiling underslick below. Glenda and I paddled mightily with draw strokes to bring us out of a broadside slip, but it was no use. The prow swung around sharply and the three of us were flipped into the air like twigs.

The world was an upside-down nightmare as my body was tumbled along by the raging current. I came to the surface sputtering and gasping for breath. Glenda cleared water at almost the same instant and our eyes met as we swung frantically from side to side, looking for our little daughter. Terror widened the eyes of my wife. Even the roar of the rapids now spilling around us couldn't dull her scream. "Lynette—Lynette, where is she?"

My heart was trying to burst out of my chest. All I remember is that 7 or 8 seconds flashed by while I had no conscious thought of what to do; there was no time, no going back, no chance to search. The whole world was spinning madly downhill.

Then something brushed against my thrashing legs and I thrust them upward with all my strength. Up bobbed Lynette, sputtering and paddling furiously. I boosted her halfway up the overturned hull, holding her with one hand and keeping my balance with the other as we dropped through another chute of white water. Glenda was trying desperately to guide us toward the flashing shore. I was getting tired.

Then Vance and Val sped up from behind. The kayak had bounced over the falls and stayed upright, and they were now paddling powerfully in our direction. As they swept by, Vance plucked Lynette off the hull of the canoe with the same deft motion he might have used to net a fighting salmon.

The current finally slowed and we all were able to struggle to shore. Val quickly silenced her sister's frightened sobs, and Vance was soon swimming in and out from shore, retrieving the domestic flotsam as it swept by—a paddle, some clothes, and a knapsack that had come loose from its lashings during the pounding. We bailed out the canoe and sat down to take stock. There were only a few odds and ends missing. Certainly, the situation wasn't desperate, although everyone but the near-victim knew how close death had been. It had been our first real moment of danger or difficulty and we didn't want to let it ruin the outing.

"We" is not completely accurate. Glenda had been uneasy since we had first felt the strong pull of the Klamath current. She was more than that now. She agreed to continue since we were trapped far below the road by the steep canyon walls, and it would have been a long walk out. But she insisted that we were to be extra cautious and that we would stop at the first safe take-out.

The sun was beginning to dry things out, and we were soon repacked and ready to shove off once more. I looked around for Lynette and spotted her 200 yards downstream and trudging determinedly along the shore. I called out that we were ready to go again. "You're not getting me back in that boat again," she replied matter-of-factly, her little chin thrust out boldly. "I'm going to walk the rest of the way." It was like flipping the petcock on a pressure cooker. All of us doubled over with laughter.

The next few miles were easy and peaceful until a sharp curve brought us to a wide but shallow crossing strewn with rocks. Halfway through the crossing, there was a grinding screech as we hung up on a rock. Glenda and I vaulted out on the downstream side to swing the boat off the rock, but then the fast water knocked our feet loose and pushed the boat off the rock all in one motion. The boat began speeding straight toward a long jagged snag while we thrashed along beside it, trying to keep up with it, protect it, and stay on our feet all at the same time. I shoved the boat away from the snag at the last moment, then we were out again in the current, which was swept with undertows and crosscurrents as it drove into a sharp bank before plunging into an even steeper box canyon than that which now flanked us. Lynette was still in the boat, lifejacket securely fastened.

I was desperately worried. Either we reached shore within the next few seconds or we and the canoe and Lynette would be swept helplessly into the seething rapids and rocks that I knew must lie below. I struggled wildly with the racing boat, but it was Glenda, mustering the kind of strength that only a maternal instinct yields in moments of danger to offspring, who lunged for a drooping willow branch, hung on, and finally pulled us into a narrow side-eddy. Val and Vance made it to shore intact, but only after some powerful paddling.

There was no way out now but to line the boats back upriver with long ropes brought along for just such an emergency, tied fore and aft to the canoe and kayak. Rocks bruised our ankles and thorns of blackberry bushes tore at our faces and arms as we proceeded along the shore. Vance drew on an unknown reserve of strength, lifting the girls and his mother over ledges and up steep banks and then helping me with the boats. Several hours later we crumpled, exhausted, at the foot of a path leading upward to the Klamath River Lodge. We rented one of the cabins and called an end to this madness.

Later, after a shower and hot meal, Glenda and I sank wearily into chairs on the patio, drinking in the beauty of dusk falling on the warm fragrant air of the canyon. The fear and agony of the afternoon were only secretly satisfying memories now. Inside, there was happy laughter. The girls were playing bingo with a crude combination of acorns and scrap paper fashioned by Lynette. Afterward, our exhausted son told them bedtime stories. They were suddenly close again and seemed years younger.

Glenda and I exchanged a knowing glance. Words were needless. The togetherness was back. We had lost a puzzled, frustrated boy and gained, instead, a young man—strong, sound, and mighty good in a pinch. Our daughters, too, seemed more vital and valuable, needed and happy again. A slight squeeze, a smile of contentment, were our eloquent speeches of reassurance.

We had been in over our heads on the angry Klamath and we both knew it now. It is no place for inexperienced explorers in an open canoe. But our escape had been from more than swirling waters. It was from a past too long etched in distraction and distress. And we could thank the wild waters for that. The last soft rays of the setting sun touched off the first notes of nature's nocturnal chorus. This was the rebirth we had sought.

A few runs through short, bouncy rapids of
California's rivers will hook you on this exciting
outdoor sport.

Preparing
Your Escape

BOATING through isolated wilderness or even along the peaceful farm-dotted countryside nearer civilization sounds very romantic and adventurous. And so it is. However, there are also several kinds of back-bending labor and commonplace drudgery associated with river touring and camping. Portages may sound heroically poetic, but they are in reality demanding physical exertions. This is all by way of cautioning the reader and potential river boater (1) that moderation is but another word for wisdom; don't try to tackle more than your experience and endurance will permit. (2) While there are few who don't find river boating's magnetism irresistible, there are, nevertheless, a few. You may be one who will not like the rough-hewn lifestyle and hard work involved in touring the countryside by canoe, kayak, or raft.

The best way to find out is, of course, to try it, and I urge beginners to start out by renting a canoe for a day or two on one of the growing number of rivers where rental concessions have sprung up—the Russian, Sacramento, American, and Colorado, to name four. Rent, not buy. Those who have taken the whole plunge, outfitting completely before even the first trial run and then finding life on the river too rigorous, have also taken an economic bath in the process. Rentals have another benefit; they give the greenhorn a chance to try out different boat models, giving him a better idea of what he wants for himself and why.

It is difficult to pin down just where the preparation for a river tour really starts, though certainly picking the boat is up somewhere toward the head of the list. The following pages will explain how to pick your boat and most of the other necessary preparatory steps to get you properly equipped, trained, guided, and motivated to enjoy the unique rewards of river cruising.

PICKING THE BOAT

From the time of the first crude dugouts to the bold but fragile birch-bark creations of the American Indian and the succeeding wood-and-canvas, aluminum, and fiberglass models, the design of the canoe has remained basically unaltered. Its shape gives the craft the versatility that makes it so desirable and useful: Pointed at both ends, it slices cleanly and quietly through the water, making only a narrow part and leaving just a trace of wake in its path. It is, of course, exaggeration to say that you could float a canoe in heavy dew, but the point is obvious. It draws very little water, skimming through shallows barely more than ankle deep if the load is modest and its balancing proper. And, best of all, the graceful design of the canoe permits maximum propulsion with only minimum effort.

Versatility is the craft's byword. It can be paddled, poled, sailed, or even powered with a small outboard motor. The more streamlined the design, the more swift its speed. The same increasing length-to-width ratio also enhances the craft's stability, its holding and handling capabilities, and its speed potential.

Basically, there are but two canoe designs: the double-pointer and the square stern. The square stern model is specifically designed to accommodate small outboard motors and is ideal for trolling or upriver work on major rivers. It has a distinct drawback, however, in downriver boating. Often, in downriver boating, there is a need to poise just at the brink of a chute, back-sculling briskly to gain a split second or two while you pick a path through what lies below. It is at times like this that the force of the river piling up against the flat form of the stern makes the job just that much tougher. This difficulty can quickly become something more pronounced if you're in big, fast-moving water and suddenly come upon an unexpected obstacle.

Canoes run in popular lengths from 13 to 20 feet. There are

This is the gear the author chose for his family's
first river adventure.

exceptions at both ends of the scale, of course—the lower end for closed white-water canoes (one-passenger jobs not unlike a kayak) and the upper end for the river freighters still popular in Canada's North Country. The factory models come equipped with built-in seats, popular with most occasional canoers. Veteran white water rats often prefer to remove the seats, paddling from a kneeling position—the classic stance—and using a specially placed thwart for a back rest. This is not recommended for the fun lovers. The pros point out that it gives their bodies more freedom to alter strokes and position quickly in response to the demands of the water conditions. For the inexperienced or poorly conditioned boater, however, the kneeling position can bring excruciating pain to unused thigh and trunk muscles.

I would recommend starting out with a sturdy aluminum canoe. There are at least half a dozen different reliable makes, most of them equal in quality and performance so long as you make sure that the thickness of the metal shell is at least .53 gauge or more. My favoritism for aluminum is anchored in practicality. It takes a while to work the kinks out in this sport, and while you're working them out for yourself and your partner, you are more than likely to be working them into the underside of your craft. An aluminum craft takes these knocks in stride and can be quickly pounded back into good shape when the dents or the creases are a bit too deep. The aluminum canoe also has a fine weight-to-length ratio.

A nice length for canoe camping is 16 or 17 feet, big enough to handle plenty of gear and yet not too cumbersome in challenging white water. You can get longer models, but they are a bit bulky and slow to respond in tough going. These longer models also present two or three more feet that must be twisted through some of the tight corners of white-water running.

Our selection of a 15-foot aluminum Starcraft was more the result of a fine bargain than ideal selection, though we have never been unhappy with its performance or endurance. Also by shopping accident, we wound up with a deep, smooth-water lake keel—the strong thin edge of metal that juts downward from the middle of the hull to prevent slippage across the top of the water and to add to the craft's responsiveness to turning efforts. Actually, a shoe keel—stubbier, almost rounded, and much stronger—is recommended for river boats. With it, you are more likely to slide over a rock, rather than catching it with the more deeply protruding lake keel. Our family has made the progression now to a passionate craving for a sleek, two-man, European-style fiberglass canoe (C-2) for more daring white-water work. But had we started out with such a fine craft, I'm afraid we would have had patches on the patches by now.

As a second boat for our family of five, we selected an inflatable two-man kayak of rubberized fabric. Virtually unsinkable, this French-made craft, called a Sevylor, has many advantages—and several offsetting disadvantages as well, at least for river touring. On the plus side, there is almost nothing in the way of white water that even a greenhorn can't negotiate in this type of kayak. I've seen them take a punishing white water trough sideways and bounce through it like a feather. There have been many times when we've been able to take friends through water otherwise far beyond their capability to handle. An equally important plus factor—in fact, the real selling point for us—is that we could carry the deflated craft in our automobile trunk, and we could even back-pack its surprising 22-pound weight for some high-mountain lake trolling.

The disadvantages of the inflatable kayak are just as noteworthy. It is a rather cumbersome craft in the water as far as speed is concerned; when you hit slow water, only vigorous tandem paddling will keep you up with a canoe. In fact, the *drifting* Starcraft has kept pace with the Sevylor when its passengers were paddling strenuously. Additionally, the kayak has virtually no cargo capacity, a rather severe limiting factor when camping.

Rigid-frame kayaks and decked canoes have all the range of the open canoe, plus an ability to go where open canoes dare not venture. They are also more maneuverable than canoes and deliver a more personal experience with the river. But they have space limits which would force the river-touring family to buy one for each member, both a cost and transporting disadvantage. Fiberglass models are the most practical. They cost less, weigh less, and last longer with less care. Wood-and-canvas styles are too heavy, too susceptible to rapid damage, and too hard to repair. Many kayak clubs have their own molds and will loan them to a newcomer and help him make his own fiberglass craft, which would mean a considerable savings.

Rafts, of course, are one step further in regard to boating range.

They can go anywhere that either canoes or kayaks can, plus they can tackle hundreds of miles of rivers strictly off limits to other craft because of impassable obstacles. The one- or two-man soft rafts or rubber dinghies are inexpensive and lightweight for carrying, but their lack of rigidity leaves them with limited maneuverability—a distinct hazard in heavy rapids marked with sharp rocks that can easily tear the flexible fabric.

Bigger rafts for four, six, or eight passengers are equipped with rowing frames that make them a most seaworthy and maneuverable craft in any water. The huge neoprene rafts, both pontoon and flat belly models, are ideal for *real* wild-river running, such as on the Green, Snake, and Upper Colorado rivers. Eight-man rafts are in popular commercial use on the South Fork of the American, the Stanislaus, and the Klamath rivers in California. The one major drawback of rafts, of course, is their bulky size. What makes them great for sliding over tumultuous chutes and rapids, makes them slow to propel in slack or slow-moving water. They should not be mixed with canoe or kayak parties because they can't keep up the pace, and they are not suited to flat and peaceful rivers unless there is a swift current, such as on the Sacramento. Their cargo-carrying ability, however, is most helpful, and some large canoe or kayak parties detail rafts on a lag-along basis for extended trips where car shuttle of gear is impractical.

The care of any type of boats, like any maintenance program, prolongs their life and enhances their appearance. Here are some very basic steps: When storing a rigid-frame boat, such as a canoe or kayak, care should be taken to suspend it in a web or slings. The boat can be hoisted on a pulley system and hung from the garage rafters or it can be snuggled up to a garage wall or fence with slings around bow, stern, and amidships to spread the stress. If stored outside, say in a narrow sideyard, canoes and kayaks should be placed upside down to avoid water storage and the wear it would cause to the finish. If a sling or suspension hookup isn't possible, the boat can be propped on a rack of two sawhorses, but care should be taken to secure the craft and the sawhorses against falling.

To preserve the finish, aluminum boats should be scrubbed thoroughly at season's end with diluted household ammonia or cleanser, rinsed off, and then coated once or twice with car wax. Any heavy gouge marks should be filed smooth before cleaning.

Fiberglass boats should be scrubbed with a soap solution, rinsed, and then coated with car wax. Wooden boats with a painted finish need only a good scrubbing with soap and a fresh-water rinse. All rafts or rubber kayaks should be washed with soapy solution, thoroughly rinsed, and then stretched out to dry completely before storage.

Picking the Paddles

There are as many styles, lengths, and wood types in paddles as there are different kinds of razors and blades. And since paddles are presumably your sole source of propulsion, it is important that you choose them carefully and knowledgeably.

Experts are divided in their preferences among maple, spruce, and ash paddles. Maple is preferred by some because it is both springy and tough. Its disadvantage, though, is its weight, which is significant when you consider that an average paddler may take as many as 5,000 strokes a day. Planing down the thickness of the blade can help overcome this weight problem. Ash, another of the hardwoods, is lighter than maple and has more spring for thrust at the end of the stroke. It is also less prone to warp than maple but not quite so durable. Spruce paddles are even lighter than ash, and while excellent for most lake work, they are not suited to the more extreme pressures present in either heavy waves or rapids.

The one paddle prized by all experts is a handcrafted laminated paddle of white ash, with a wider than standard blade (no more than 7 inches) and a square, racing-style tip. The lamination gives the paddle great strength without excessive weight, and the wider and squared tip gives the paddle a bigger bite for more thrust and maneuvering potential.

Even more important than the weight and spring of a paddle is the grain of its wood. Just as a baseball player is careful to select a bat with a properly close and straight grain, a canoeist must examine his paddle for flaring or irregular grains not facing the direction of the blade's flat surface. You should also watch out for knot marks in the wood. These irregularities are weak points and are sure to crack under stress—the worst possible time, of course.

The bow paddle should reach no higher than the paddler's chin when stood on end—the paddle, not the paddler. The length of the stern paddle, on the other hand, should reach somewhere from the eyebrows to the top of the head. The extra length is needed for the stern man because of the greater maneuvering the stern position demands.

Blade styles include the beavertail, voyageur, Indian, and racing models. The beavertail is the wider of these blades and therefore has a more pronounced purchase per stroke. It is a good touring paddle and is better suited to huskier paddlers, preferably in the stern. The voyageur is the more common blade style, a modification between the bulky beavertail and slim-contour Indian blade, and is probably the best bet for casual paddlers. The slimmer Indian blade is especially good for children or adults with a slight build and a small grip. The racing blade is, of course, for more energetic work, with its square end and wide blade design for maximum propulsion. The only drawback of the racer is that it takes a muscular, well-conditioned athlete to handle it with precision and effect. The most common paddle grips are the pear, modified pear, T, and modified T. Select the one that feels best to you.

Many of the same principles apply to selection of the double-bladed kayak paddles. Both the need for good, tight grip and the ability to bear heavy bursts of stress put maximum demands upon the long, narrow shaft of the kayak paddle. Wood grain, again, is a matter of real importance. Some kayakers are switching to the new line of fabricated double-blades, the ones with a sturdy aluminum alloy shaft and stiff plastic blades. They are not so handsome as the more traditional maple or ash paddle, but they are almost resistant to wear. Their one obvious drawback is the unusual thickness of the shaft, making it rather awkward and bulky to grip tightly, especially for women and children.

Raft paddles are another story. The best piece of advice I can give you about the tiny light-gauge aluminum paddles that come with the popular two-man rafts is to recycle them at the nearest ecology center. They are useless in fast water, cannot withstand even the stress of moderate stroking, and, once snapped, take a rough edge that makes them potentially dangerous in an upset. In addition, most of them are so short you find it hard to reach water with them and so narrow that when you do, the results are hardly worth the trouble. Short, light canoe paddles are a better bet for small rafts.

The bigger rafts are in a league all their own. They are equipped with rowing frames, and the "paddles" that provide maneuvering power are really long slender oars. Lighter and thinner than the regular rowboat variety, these crucial tools place less emphasis on lightness or spring and more on plain brute strength. The hardwoods, especially maple and oak, are good bets for the oars for large rafts. Sanding or planing will help cut down any weight problems.

There is one more vital aspect that all paddles for all types of river craft have in common—the need for emergency back-up. The boater who embarks on a touring episode, no matter how short or mild, without an extra paddle is likely to find himself up that well-known creek and in plenty of trouble. At the very least, it can mean a long and slow drift to your destination or a premature take-out. More likely it will mean very real danger. Breaks usually come in moments of stress in heavy rapids, and there can't be a worse time to run out of steering control. Always pack an extra paddle, and make sure it is securely lashed into the boat.

The key to prolonged paddle life is good maintenance. Don't leave wet paddles out in the hot sun, and take care to hang them up when you get home rather than just flinging them into the nearest corner. In addition, keep them well-sanded and coated with linseed oil or marine varnish from season to season. Never varnish the grip; it should be oiled. With this minimum of care, your paddles will be constant and trusty companions.

Mapping, Scouting, and Classifying the Rivers

The following classification of rivers for boaters was devised by the American White Water Affiliation. I have followed this rating system throughout my evaluation of California rivers and the writing of this guide book. You will also find the ratings in a growing number of monthly river-boating magazines and the few good guide books available. This system is used widely to describe river conditions and boating ratings throughout this country and for many Canadian and European waters as well. Keep in mind that the rating measures the river, not the skills of the boater:

RATING GUIDE FOR BOATERS

CLASS I (very easy)

Waves small, regular; riffles only, no rapids; passages clear and wide.

CLASS II (easy)

Waves and rapids of medium difficulty; passages clear and wide; some small obstructions; spraydeck useful.

CLASS III (moderately difficult)

Waves numerous, high, irregular; rocks, eddies, difficult rapids; passages clear but narrow, requiring expertise in maneuver; preliminary scouting of passages needed; spraydeck needed.

CLASS IV (difficult)

Waves powerful and irregular; dangerous rocks, boiling eddies, long and very demanding rapids; passages difficult to see, require powerful and precise maneuvering; scouting mandatory first time; spraydeck essential.

CLASS V (very difficult)

Very difficult, long, and very violent rapids, following each other almost without interruption;; riverbed extremely obstructed; big drops, violent current, very steep gradient; scouting difficult, essential every passage; spraydeck essential.

CLASS VI (extremely difficult)

Difficulties of Class V carried to extremes of navigability; nearly impossible and very dangerous; suitable only for teams of experts and only then at favorable water levels and after very close study of water.

Classes I and II water can be handled by open canoes; but only experienced boaters should try Class III waters in open craft, and they should do so only when they are assured of time for bailing. Class IV water—and beyond—is safe only for *skilled* boaters in kayaks, the popular European C-1 or C-2 decked canoes, or rafts with rowing frames.

In addition to reading a book such as this and following its rating guide, there are many other ways of checking out the possibilities of boating a particular stream or river. For example, inasmuch as most rivers in the state flow through canyons, they are also paralleled by major roads for a good part of their length. Thus, one of the first steps in selecting a river is to scout it out by driving along it, with occasional stops to hike over a bank for a better look at a hidden bend.

The next step is to check with gas station attendants, resort personnel, etc., to try to find someone of experience who has already made the run, preferably within the same season, and to get from him all of the up-to-date information on dangers and obstacles. You can't depend solely on this information, however, any more than you could rely entirely on what I have to say later in this book. The rivers change some from year to year, depending on the intensity of the winter storms they just survived. New boulders may have rolled into the riverbed, or new channels may have been sliced and scoured by heavy flooding. Don't be

Class I

Class II

Class III

Class IV

Class V

Class VI

shy about asking questions; we have found members of the boating clan always eager to share their experiences.

Another resource is the United States Geological Survey in Menlo Park and San Francisco, which offers for sale a complete set of quadrangle topographical maps of all of the state. Although the agency is still completing a changeover to standardized 7½-minute quadrangles, with a very detailed scale of 2⅝ inches to the mile, you can obtain a nearly full set of 15-minute maps with a scale of 1 inch to the mile. The contour lines on these maps, marking the elevation above sea level, give an accurate picture of the surrounding landscape and therefore the gradient patterns of a river. Some maps feature contours every 5 feet, others 20, and still others 25. The trick is in learning how to read the contours accurately. Most of the USGS people will be glad to set aside a few minutes for a detailed explanation.

The markings of a map also begin to take on new meaning and clarity once you have read a river by map and then traversed it by boat. You find, for example, that map legends for big and small falls and big and small rapids are usually wrong or misleading. You also discover that the width of a river on a map can provide you with precisely accurate information. Where the river narrows down to a pencil-thin line, you can be sure to hit rapids or a drop. And where there is a wide blue meandering pattern, you can be just as sure to find extremely slow-moving water. Finally, you learn that map gradients of 10 feet per mile or less, over a long river run, put the water in the Class I range, while a gradient of 10–20 feet is Class II. As a rule, with open canoes, I would approach with considerable caution any run with a gradient above 35 feet to the mile. A gradient of 50 feet per mile is toward the danger limit for an open canoe, even for experts.

Of course, this kind of generalizing can be dangerous, for it matters little if 8 miles of a river are Class I when 200 yards in the middle are suddenly Class V. That is why it is best to get information from a source that knows the river first-hand. And that is also why beginners should start out the right way, by joining the Sierra Club and one of its growing river-touring sections or the American Canoe Association. Both have excellent training and river-rating programs. Both also feature a wonderful series of group runs during the different seasons. There are also many Red Cross, YMCA, or Boy Scout groups that sponsor canoe training and safety classes, or will upon sufficient demand. The best investment you can make, from every conceivable standpoint, is to take one of these classes. Absolutely nothing substitutes for this kind of training and experience. It can mean the difference between a truly magical outdoor experience and a painful and premature end to an otherwise perfectly safe, yet thrilling, hobby.

Reading the Water

The only valid textbook for learning how to read water signs is the river itself. It is one thing to read about a boil, a slick, a cascade rapids, or a whirlpool, but it means nothing without first-hand observation. Still, the following background information may be helpful:

A sharp underwater rock splits the water, forming a V that points upstream. Avoid such splits, or if they can't be missed altogether, ride only the outside edge of the V.

A trailing V ripple pointing upstream can also indicate a subsurface snag that is angled downstream. The same obstruction angled upstream—much more dangerous—would throw up a downstream V. Avoid such signs at all cost—unless you are heading into a rapids, in which case a slick or long downstream-pointing V in the midst of high waves often signals a haven for safe passage.

A large smooth underwater rock pushes up a boil, and the size of the boil above the water indicates the nearness of the rock to the surface. Most boils should be bypassed.

White water may sound and look very romantic, but it is strictly to be loved at a very long arm's length. Only experience will reveal the difference between white water that is just water turbulence and not too dangerous, and white water thrust up by dangerous obstructions. The best rule is to avoid white water wherever possible; it is most likely to be a sign of sharp rocks or snags dangerously close to the surface, with the added possibility of powerful current.

The presence of "white horses," the frothy streamers of water flung up by conflict between the current and an obstruction, generally signal the need for a pull out to scout what lies ahead. You will come to know the difference between the "haystacks" caused by obstructions and the standing waves caused when fast surface water slams into slower, deeper water. Canoes tend to ship water in the latter because the foamy waves are too aerated and don't have enough water for buoyancy. Both paddlers should shift to the middle of the boat in such water to raise the bow and stern.

If you decide to proceed through white water of any kind, aim for the edge of combers, quartering into or out of them rather than slicing straight into them. Of course, conditions downstream may sometimes dictate a straight-on approach. In these cases, slip down into a kneeling stance. You don't have to pray (though I recommend it when the risk appears high), but by kneeling, you lower the boat's center of gravity and greatly enhance its stability in the water. You can ride out nearly any kind of water once you get the rhythm and feel of the boat and master the trick of keeping in balance and harmony with its wildest gyrations.

Rapids should be run with just enough speed to stay ahead of the current and to maintain control of the steerage. The rougher the water, the less speed is desirable; for it is crucial that you have time to scout and maneuver. In such situations, we have found back-sculling useful for breaking speed and gaining time. In fact, we've often back-paddled through an entire run of rapids. This kind of stroke also helps keep the prow of the craft from nosing under high waves.

There are two schools of thought about who assumes command of the boat in such situations. Normally, the stern man is the boss, but in white water the position of the bowman and the likelihood that he'll spot any trouble first would seem to make him the natural captain. Whichever school you follow, settle on it ahead of time. Nothing is more foolhardy, or dangerous, than having a divided command at a time when split-second decisions are necessary.

We found it most reliable to let the more experienced man take the bow and command of the boat. His sternman should be prepared to steady the craft on demand, so that the bowman can stand for a better look at what is downstream. While the bowman gets up, with his feet balanced close to the center line and pointing in, the sternman should stay low and maintain balance by placing his paddle deep into the water and flat to the line of the boat. The paddle then serves as an extra deep keel, preventing slide and flip. This maneuver should only be practiced in relatively calm water, of course.

While most rapids give off a thunderous warning roar, there are some that do not. We have been scooped into a steep, mid-stream, 4-foot falls without hearing so much as a whisper of danger until it was too late. More cautious scouting procedures could have prevented the problem, of course.

Waterfalls, too, are often capricious in their vocal patterns. While most can be heard for hundreds of yards downstream, they are sometimes not heard at all upstream of their precipitous drops until you are at the very brink. Here again, advance knowledge of the terrain is crucial.

There are very few whirlpools on California rivers, at least none big enough to capture a canoe. But back-boils and back-eddies are numerous, and they are strong enough to upset canoes unless the paddlers are prepared. When they spot a reverse thrust, they should kneel low in the boat. Then the bowman must make strong and sweeping draw strokes on the opposite side of the eddy current while the sternman applies powerful forward thrusts on the same side or a reverse pushover draw on the opposite side from the bowman.

These thoughts and general guidelines represent only the high-lights of some of the more common water types with which a paddler must become familiar for a safe and pleasurable trip. I must emphasize again that no one should start out river running without first having completed a canoe safety and training course. This seems like a natural time also to drop in another reminder on one of the rules of safe boating, especially for open craft, which are much more vulnerable to taking high waves over the gunwhales. One of the paddler's worst enemies is a lack of balance, and nothing robs him of that more quickly than shipped water sloshing back and forth and from side to side with each gyration of the current. It has been our experience that wipeouts come as often from this cause as from most of the rest of the river obstacles put together. Bailing devices, activated by foot-pump, can be picked up at most boating stores, or you can use a large plastic bleach bottle, with the cap still on and about a third of the bottom cut away. The latter makes a perfect bailer, with its handle, light weight and large size. We have been able to bail unwanted watery ballast in just a minute or so of vigorous scooping.

This mild wipeout in the Trinity River gorge is
the result of failing to read the water carefully.
Note how soggy passengers guide submerged but
floating craft from the upstream side to avoid
getting trapped between boat and obstacle. Only
the seat cushions floated free. Everything else is
securely lashed.

CARRYING THE BOAT

There are as many different ways to carry your boat as there are different vehicles on which to carry them. For passenger cars that double as recreation vehicles on weekends, we have found the adjustable, metal, car-top carriers the best—the kind that attach under the rain gutter of the roof with a strong swivel pressure clamp. A swatch of carpet over the rounded bars of the carrier will prevent noisy vibration.

The gunwhales of the canoe or kayak rest on the rounded metal bars, front and back, and heavy duck straps stretch over the hull and hold the boat down tight. It would be wise to have a new set of extra-large rivets clamped into these pieces of webbing; the smaller ones that come with the set tend to pull right through the webbing material. Other ways to make the boat snug against the carry bars are to loop rubber inner tubes over the ends of the bars. The tension of the tubes as they are stretched over the inverted hull is more than enough to secure the craft to the bars. Thick rubber car-top carrier luggage straps, with metal S-hooks on each end, are another adequate substitute. It is also important to purchase S-hook tie-down clamps to anchor the bow and stern to the car bumpers. The clamps should be tight to prevent boat slippage on the bars.

Lashing the boat atop the carrier bars with ropes is not recommended simply because it is time consuming and troublesome; inevitably, ropes have to be cinched up at least once or twice during a trip. I would also caution you against using the suction-type car-top carriers to hold your boat. They just don't have the grip necessary to do the job. Heavy crosswinds against the length of the boat are likely to cost you a very expensive outfit when—notice I didn't say if—those suction cups pull free.

Kayak-carrying rigs involve wooden or molded convex yokes atop cartop carriers into which the kayak can be placed right side up. The craft are then tied securely with S-hook tie-down clamps. Some families fashion their own trailer rigs with either V-bars or convex molds to hold the boats. Some even go into a tandem arrangement for four to six craft, stacking them atop one another on welded metal frames.

Rafts, of course, pose no real carrying problems, but if you choose to stretch them flat in the trunk to make maximum use of space, care should be taken to avoid sharp objects or edges that could wear through and puncture the rubber shell.

SHUTTLING

There are so many different possibilities and needs for return transportation to your car from the downstream take-out that it is impossible to recommend just one simple method. The following suggestions will consider most of the options, placing top emphasis on economy and diminishing importance on reliability, convenience, and comfort.

The most inexpensive method for the one-car family to get back to their launching place is hitchhiking. We have done this many times and have rarely been delayed and never stranded. A fair-sized lettered card, "Canoeing: Need Ride Back Upriver," will help overcome the fears of most motorists and excite the curiosity of others. It is generally best to have the man do the hitchhiking, and someone should always remain with the boat and gear. Also, study the road maps closely to become completely familiar with the routes you should take. While this system has never failed us, it can put time constraints on you for finishing your trip early enough to leave plenty of daylight for your thumbing.

Some runs, such as the upper Merced River, the Trinity, the South Fork of the Eel, the Stanislaus, and the Russian have put-ins and take outs along major routes that offer bus transportation. Bus schedules should be checked before embarking and take-out time designed accordingly. It would be just slightly more costly to contract at the scene for an impromptu "taxi" service. Some resort owners may be interested in providing return shuttle, for a price, of course. Several times, we quickly found young men with cars or motorbikes who snapped at the chance to earn a few extra dollars. As the interest in canoeing picks up, the law of supply and demand will surely develop more of this kind of transportation service.

The ultimate convenience, independence, and reliability for a return is to have more than one car in the canoeing party. It is best, first, to unload the boats and unpack all the gear from the cars at the put-in. That way, somebody can be getting ready to launch while the pickup car is driven downstream and left at the take-out spot. Some scouting is needed to make sure you are leaving your car in a safe, legal place. It is best to park it in a yard or near some public place, after asking permission. Motels and other resorts would expect a small parking fee, but your car would be more protected there. If you are lucky enough to have a couple of drivers who aren't planning to boat, then your return shuttle is easily solved. Large canoeing groups often set up their schedules with a rotating assignment for shuttle service. That way, on overnight trips, everybody gets to do some boating.

The remaining options are more convenient, but cost is a factor. If your transportation to streamside is a camper or pickup truck and you can afford the extra cost, a small trailbike in a welded carrying frame makes an ideal shuttle vehicle. When you drop off the trailbike at the downstream end of your route, try to leave it with someone trustworthy. Failing that, the bike should be wheeled into a secure hiding spot, fastened to a tree with a case-hardened steel chain, and then camouflaged with tree limbs and leaves. We know of some energetic families who use a 10-speed bike for their shuttle. It does work the kinks out of cramped legs.

SELECTING ACCESSORIES

Endless is the list of accessories that can make boating more comfortable, but very few of them are vital. I would recommend outlays for floorboards as they save much wear and tear on the hull and keep the gear dry most of the time, to say nothing of the feet and seat if you're an amidships passenger. Carrying-yokes for easier one-man portages are also handy, since this kind of boat-carrying frees your partner to handle the rest of the gear and cuts down on unnecessary shuttles along steep portage trails. However, buy only those models that are molded to fit the shoulders. The straight, cushioned type put an excessive strain on the tricep muscles over the shoulders.

Life preservers are really more of a necessity than an accessory. No boat should be without one for each passenger. Those who are not strong swimmers should wear one at all times, and in fast water, all hands should have them on. There are the expensive jacket-type preservers and many other new models, but it's tough to beat the economy and reliability of the time-tested Mae West harnesses.

There is also an endless variety of gear bags. We started out with rubberized GI laundry bags lined with plastic garbage-can bags. To assure watertightness, both bags should be looped over in a U at the top and then tied tightly. We found, however, that the laundry bags are too thin and rip easily. A similar but better combination is a heavy, drill, ditty bag lined with the plastic garbage-can bags.

Best protection, though, comes from the rubber box-like containers used during World War II for encasing motor generators. These "black bags," as boaters call them, are available at almost all war surplus stores, some of them unused and still wrapped in the protective coating of paper and powder. The boxes taper up into a long rubber neck with a fitted lip. This neck is folded and rolled to provide complete watertight capability. Care must be taken at the start of the folding to insert the front, single edge of the neck into the folded back lip, then crease it over and over, first pushing out most of the air through one side slot. A square rubber lid then covers the folded neck and is secured by heavy drill straps.

We've put these containers to the acid test and found them absolutely perfect on the trail and in the boat. They fit nicely into a boat, measuring 20 inches across the front, 18 inches along the sides, and 14 inches in width, although you can sometimes expand that an inch or two by putting the soft compressible gear on top and squeezing down. One box can hold two rolled sleeping bags, two air mattresses, a ground sheet, and two full changes of clothes if they are laid out flat. Into another of these boxes we've packed our food, first-aid kit, mosquito netting, extra jackets, pots and pans, and extras like mosquito dope and suntan lotion.

An added advantage of the black bags is that they are already equipped with four metal rings on each base. We put these rings to excellent use by slipping the S-hooks of the car-top boat straps into them—two diagonally across the top of the box and two under the bottom. The rubber boat straps pin the boxes on either side of the center thwart for good balance and trim. Several wipe-outs with that combination didn't cost a single piece of lost gear.

Similar but smaller rubber boxes or bags are available for smaller loads. These bags have reinforced-rubber handles on the sides for carrying on short stretches. They are also equipped with long rubber straps, front and back, which are perfect for shoulder harnesses on long portages.

Some people use these smaller bags for expensive camera gear, but I've found that the bags take too long to open. Whatever it was you were interested in snapping is usually out of sight by the time you get the bag undone. A much better method, I think, is to purchase a small ammunition can from a war-surplus store. Make sure that the rubber seal around the top is not brittle or flaked and that the can is not bent so badly that the pressure lid won't clamp shut. Then line the top and bottom of the can with sponge or foam and you have a strong, watertight, and easily accessible camera case. The can isn't guaranteed to float, however, so you should lash it to the thwarts.

SELECTING THE GEAR

The primary goal in packing for a river tour, or for any other camping trip, is to cut out as much weight as possible. For that reason, we select most of our food supply from the fine line of freeze-dried foods prepared and packaged for back-packing. These freeze-dried foods are quite expensive; but they are also very convenient and generally delicious, and they permit a variety of sumptuous meals in the wilds that would otherwise be impossible. You can also make some economical substitutions, such as buying larger, less costly packages of pancake mix that needs only water and then repacking the mix into more easily carried plastic bags.

It is important to have a waterproof watch along when cooking with the dried foods, for the timing is often crucial to their succulence and flavor. A watch will also serve the vital role of estimating mileage, once you have learned the knack of correctly gauging the speed of your stroke and that of the current. Being able to judge speed and distance on a strange run can often mean the difference between reaching your destination in safe daylight or trying to make it in the dangerous half-light of dusk. This skill can also help you prepare for obstacles mentioned in a guide such as this one, which measures in river miles. You can develop this skill by timing yourself on familiar courses until you have a good idea of how many miles you can make in an hour of leisurely stroking or rapid paddling on slow current or fast.

If you plan to do most of your boating in mild weather, I would recommend for your bedding the 3-pound dacron mummy-style bags, because they roll up into a very compact and light-weight package. A flannel liner will provide added warmth when the temperature dips. Being city softies and never really having learned to fit the contour of our backsides around rocks and twigs, we also invested in a set of the heavy, rubberized-fabric air mattresses. They were a weight and packing problem, but we learned to appreciate them, nonetheless.

Some people prefer down-filled sleeping bags, but when buying a family set, the price tag can mount rather quickly. Too, there is very little need in California for the below-zero protection that this type of bag offers. Flannelette pajamas are a cheap substitute when the mercury falls. A sheet of polyethylene plastic makes a fine ground sheet, and mosquito nets have come in handy several times, though it takes some ingenuity to find the right kind of props on a gravel bar to string the nets up. Instead of using one net to a bag—that is, lengthwise—we doubled up and used the netting to cover only the upper part of two bodies. After weighting the corners of the net with rocks or shoes, we were pretty near invincible to the blood-thirsty little pests.

I have never found axes or saws very necessary on our river tours, for there has always been plenty of driftwood which is easily broken into campfire-size pieces. However, a fold-blade saw doesn't weigh much, and I've had use for one occasionally. If you prefer a hatchet or axe, don't scrimp on money. Any hatchet under $7 is not likely to keep a usable edge, and the same is true of axes under $15. You're also likely to end up with a split handle as well.

Watertight match containers are a must on a boating tour. There are also special waterproof matches available in most sporting goods stores, together with watertight containers to add double protection. Two sets of these—one in each of the two watertight gear bags, just in case—are a sensible precaution.

Other necessary camping odds and ends range from personal items—toothbrush and paste, washcloth, towel, hand soap, and toilet tissue—to things like a first-aid kit, a compass, a signaling whistle, a good sheath knife, suntan lotion, and a skin cream if your skin tends to chap and irritate after repeated dunkings and dryings. The suntan lotion is no luxury item; the combination of direct sunlight and reflections off the water and boat is like getting a triple dose of sun all at once. It is wise to have had gradual exposures to the sun in the weeks before you make your trip; painful sunburns, as we have found out, can ruin a trip.

SELECTING CLOTHING

Depending upon the altitude and the temperature patterns of the area you will cover, it is usually best to dress with several layers of clothing in preparation for the variety of weather and temperature you are likely to encounter—from the chill of early morning or late evening to the heat of midday. Shorts or swimming trunks, light cotton or woolen teeshirts, and woolen socks (for good insulation) make an ideal inner lining to shed down to later in the day as the sun warms the air. A fairly heavy woolen sweater or jacket, and drill or cotton slacks will serve well as the outside layer. For those hardy souls who engage in wintertime boating, wetsuits are sometimes most useful; for a dunking at 40 degrees can be a most discomforting experience. Tight clothes may be very chic at home but they are a curse in a canoe, where they tend to cut off circulation and increase irritation. Loose-fitting pants are especially important.

A soft, wide-brimmed cloth or felt hat, which can be pulled down tight on the forehead, is a necessity to protect against glare and heat. Polaroid sunglasses are worth the investment, since they are by far the most effective glare reducers and will make scouting the water—surface and sub-surface—much easier and safer. However, you should be sure to get them fitted with head straps, or an expensive pair of glasses will end up on the bottom of some river.

As for footwear, I've found it most practical to shun heavy rubber-soled boots in favor of light canvas deck shoes. Back country voyageurs would frown at such an idea; but so long as you'll encounter only mild weather and relatively undemanding portages, the lighter shoe will be adequate. The canvas shoes also provide a better grip both on the floor of the boat and on rocky stream bottoms. They dry out quicker, too, after a dunking and add up to more comfortable footwear that way as well.

The Rivers

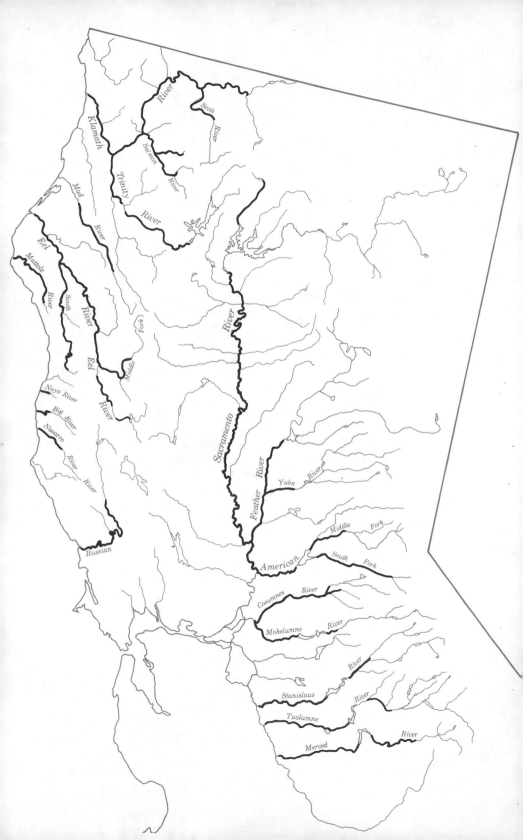

The Last Great
Wild Rivers

The Klamath River

(190 miles • CLASS I-IV)

THE Klamath springs from the snow-clad peaks on the eastern side of the Oregon Cascades, above Upper Klamath Lake, and it courses more than 75 miles before it becomes prime California canoe water below Copco Lake's Iron Gate Dam. The mighty Colorado is the only other California river that originates beyond the state's boundaries.

The Klamath has many faces. Rocky, arid canyons stare down at it from the upper end of the Central Valley; deep, isolated gorges mark the path of its midsection near Happy Camp and Orleans; and, finally, the undulating mountains of the Coast Range follow it down to the jeweled Pacific. The barren ridges that flank its upper course are studded with yucca, buck brush, and the like. As it nears the end of its vibrant journey, remnants of the primeval redwoods stand by its shores.

Gold miners have taken a fortune from its gravel bars, and lumbermen have raped much of its forest-carpeted watershed—both leaving a checkerboard of desecration. Yet, there is still enough rugged beauty and isolation along the path of the Klamath to attract those still appreciative of the serenity and inspiration wild country affords. Mother Nature's wondrous recuperative powers have begun finally to thrust up ensigns of green through the barren gravel dunes that spewed from the gold dredges. And in the harvested forest lands, where once there was nothing but ugly scars, oak, maple, flowering dogwood, pepperwood, and many of their colorful cousins have begun to cover the riverbanks. Even more remarkable, there are still places along the Klamath where small gold nuggets can be panned from the gravel, where the rugged vista of rocky gorge and the gentle fragrance of forest meld together in undisturbed beauty, where the river still asserts its timeless character.

For the boater, the Klamath offers an exciting variety of water conditions, from the heavy flow of April and May to the comparatively peaceful roll of summer, fall, and the first weeks of winter. During this long season, commercial rafters still ply sections of the river, and experienced kayak paddlers and beginning and experienced canoeists find challenging runs all along the river's course. But between January and April, the wild torrential floods on the river rival the power and danger of the Snake, the Green, and the upper Colorado Rivers.

The following are the more popular runs for the 190-mile stretch of the Klamath from Interstate Highway 5 to the ocean:

Interstate 5 to Horse Creek
(29 miles • CLASS III • Running Time 7 hours)
USGS 15 minute quadrangle maps
"Hornbrook" and "Condrey Mountain"

• Some boaters put in just below Iron Gate Dam for an extra 8 miles of running, but after the spring, this section of the river is shallow and demanding in many places. It is better to join the Klamath where the Shasta River, first of the Klamath's major tributaries in the state, flows in from the south. This junction is just downstream from an excellent launching place at the Klamath River rest area, which is reached from both the on and off ramps of Interstate 5 north of Yreka. Another ideal launching place is from the Tree of Heaven campground 5 miles farther downriver.

There is no major obstacle worth a portage on this run. The descent is gradual, less than 20 feet per mile most of the way. The few big chutes and drops demand only proper and accurate water reading. Less experienced boaters should, of course, scout anything that looks beyond their capacity.

Paddlers split the flat surface of one of the Klamath River's many smooth runs between Interstate 5 and the Pacific. High water makes the winter and early spring dangerous seasons on this mighty river. Most of it is easily accessible to and safe in open canoes the remainder of the year.

If run in the afternoon, when temperatures often soar into the 90s, sun-glasses—polaroid lenses, preferably—help take the blinding glare off the water, permitting safe visual scouting and much sharper sub-surface vision.

While Highway 96 follows the river most of the way to Horse Creek, the river forms enough isolated loops, where ideal camp-sites abound, to make the route attractive. On the other hand, the nearness of Highway 96 provides complete flexibility for the run schedule and for access to shuttle cars. Every summer, the Sierra Club conducts special two-week training sessions for beginners along this upper section of the river.

Horse Creek to Seiad Valley
(*18 miles* • CLASS II–III • *Running Time 4 hours*)
USGS 15 minute quadrangle map *"Seiad Valley"*

• This portion of the Klamath is a continuation of the moderate gradient of the upper river, though some of the drops are more exaggerated and the current becomes more powerful as the river canyon narrows and the pitch increases slightly. The first stretch worthy of caution is half a mile below Horse Creek, where there is a pronounced back-eddy coming out of a deep hole on the right side of the river. There are also some sizable rocks jutting out of the water.

The river then swings left around a small bar and into a chute, which has some of the bigger waves of this section. One of the first major stands of tall evergreens on the riverbank will help to mark this spot where the river begins to narrow down. Safe passage can be made by bearing just to the right of the center slick of the chute, drawing out away from the high combers below.

Less than a quarter of a mile downstream is another powerful chute as the river does a switchback to the right. Boaters can miss the worst of the upthrust—unless they thrill to the pounding of white water—by navigating the slight slick on the far right-hand side.

A mile further on is another short, swift drop, which demands passage to the right of the small white horses that prance along the brink. A further swing to the right should follow to draw clear of another swift chute just below.

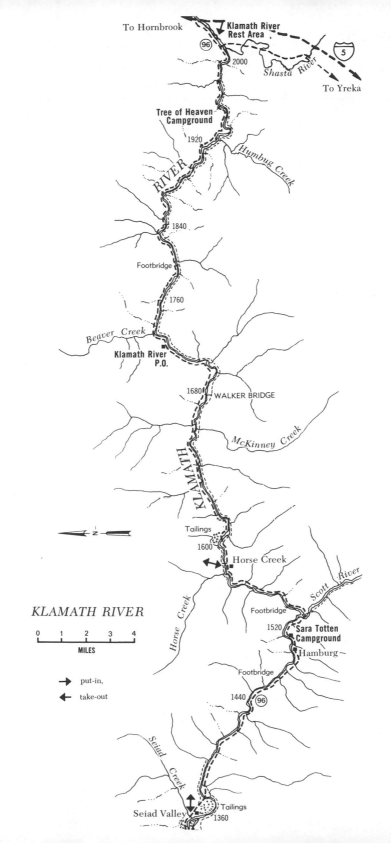

To Hornbrook

Klamath River
Rest Area

96

2000

Shasta River

To Yreka

Tree of Heaven
Campground

1920

RIVER

Humbug Creek

1840

Footbridge

1760

Beaver Creek

Klamath River
P.O.

1680 — WALKER BRIDGE

McKinney Creek

KLAMATH

N

Tailings

1600

Horse Creek

Scott River

Horse Creek

Footbridge

KLAMATH RIVER

1520

Sara Totten
Campground

Hamburg

0 1 2 3 4

MILES

Footbridge

1440 96

put-in,

take-out

Seiad Creek

Seiad Valley

Tailings

1360

You will then be gliding toward the mouth of the Scott River, a mile away. This is a great spot for anglers in the late summer, fall, or early winter when the salmon and steelhead are running. The fish stop to rest in the deep holes that the incoming Scott has scooped out of the Klamath's belly.

Half a mile downstream, despite the added head of the Scott, the river bounces over a long and very shallow ledge. The current is strong here. Boats should head into the drop just left of center, in order to clear the hog-back rock protruding from the lip. For the ensuing 50 yards, it is just a matter of keeping the prow slicing straight through the sizable and exhilarating combers.

Another half mile of eased stroking will bring you to a shallow bar and the Sara Totten Forest Service campground on the left. The far left passage offers the best clearance. At Hamburg, almost a mile beyond, is one of the run's swiftest chutes, but it is straight and offers no serious problem.

Things slacken off as the riverbed begins to spread out to match the flattening lines of the upper end of the Seiad Valley. The next 7 miles are without serious obstacle, and the river is far enough from the highway to give comparative isolation. Then, as the valley begins to spread out on the right side of the river, the tranquil pace comes to an abrupt, if brief, halt. The Klamath veers sharply left, narrowing into a chute that piles combers and troughs into a hard-hitting Class III rapids. The moderating factor here is that the course is not pocked with obstructions. High waves are the main challenge, and the center slick, right into the eye of the turbulence, is the best course. Open canoes, especially if fully loaded, are likely to ship a fair amount of water, so don't begrudge a short bailing stop.

Before reaching the next take-out, where the Klamath hooks beneath the Klamath River bridge on Highway 96, there is one other moderately demanding chute, ranging between Class II and III, depending upon the river level. The landmark here is a pronounced bared-earth slash cut above the right bank of the river. Here, the riverbed narrows quickly, squeezing its endless ribbon of water into a swift and bouncy chute. Again, the very middle of the approach is the best, in fact, the only good way through.

Below the bridge, the river swings in a broad sweep to the

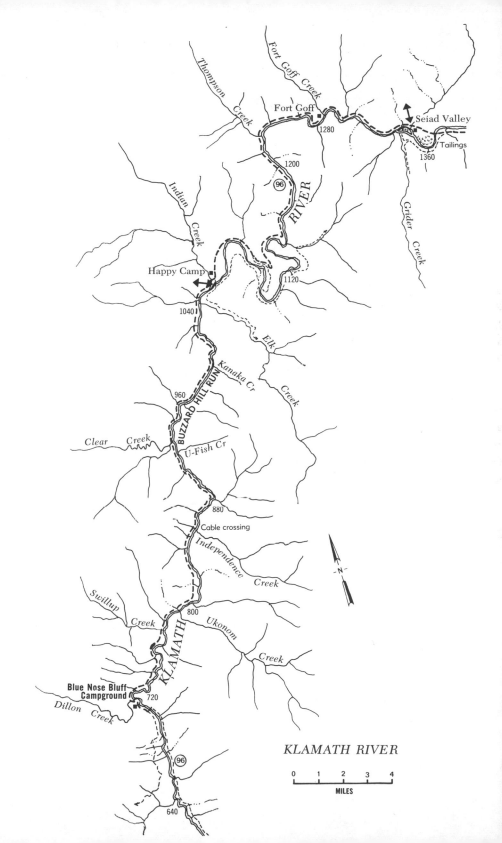

KLAMATH RIVER

0 1 2 3 4
MILES

south, hooking around a high ridge before it reaches the town of Seiad Valley. The valley floor remains flat, however, and the gradient is no different. Only two obvious turns, one going into the sweep around the ridge and the other coming back 3 miles further on, pose any difficulty.

The take-out is at Seiad Valley itself, taking the right-hand fork around a huge gravel bar to the townsite.

Seiad Valley to Happy Camp
(24 miles • CLASS II–IV • Running Time 5½ hours)
USGS 15 minute quadrangle map *"Happy Camp"*

Some of nature's finest work is on display in this stretch. The scenery changes from the pastoral beauty of the lower end of Seiad Valley to the more rugged beginnings of the Ft. Goff gorge. It climaxes with the isolated wilderness of the deep gorge through which the Klamath winds, far below the ridgeline highway. Some of the river's finest fly fishing riffles for salmon and steelhead are along this ideal overnight run. In fact, one of the river's most famous fishing guides, Jim Rhoads, uses a 12-mile piece above Happy Camp, about halfway through the gorge, as his prime float fishing water. There are also beautiful riverside campsites through most of the gorge.

As the rating indicates, this run is not suited to open canoes manned by anyone less than advanced intermediates. Predictably, it is comparatively easy going for decked canoes, kayaks, and rafts. Right below Seiad Valley, where the river arches back to the highway, it makes a short jog to the right, bouncing over a Class II chute. Navigating by the ripples and slicks pushed up by surface rocks, boaters should head for the right side of the drop for easiest passage. Thrill seekers can sweep right through the worst of it without much worry.

The going from Seiad to Ft. Goff—which has a Forest Service campground and a small liquor store and grocery on the right bank—is fairly easy; but from Ft. Goff to the beginning reaches of the gorge, there is some swift and demanding water. The first rough water is just a few hundred yards below the campground, where a sharp river-wide drop turns the Klamath into a frothy turbulence. A big boulder juts out of the current almost dead center and that is the navigational point. Boaters should key on that rock, staying only far enough to the right of center to miss it but not so far that they miss the swift but smooth slide below it. That slide will take them through all but just the moderate combers below. There is easy portage on the left should it look like too much of a hurdle.

After only an eighth of a mile of easy water for a breathing spell, there is more plunging white water. This time, however, the course is swift, straight, and comparatively trouble-free. Only high waves below have to be closely watched.

As the walls of the gorge steepen, the river begins the first of several moderate drops. Boaters can visually spot the area by a huge clear-cut timbering slash high on a peak straight downriver. The first drop is marked by a huge, flat, rock outcropping in midstream, around which the river forks. The left side is pocked with two big submerged rocks, which are dangerously close to the keel line. Best passage is on the right, staying between the outcropping and the large rocks on the bank and then hooking to the left at the base of the outcropping. A quick left-right dodge is needed to negotiate more outcroppings on the right and to catch a short slick between them and more submerged rocks in midstream.

The next 200 yards is smooth, but the river becomes extremely swift as it funnels into an 8-yard-wide racemill between pronounced solid rock walls. All but experts must maneuver carefully because of a thunderous drop below. Canoeists must stay close to the left bank and pull out in a small eddy 200 yards down from the last outcropping. Then they must either portage or let their boats down to this spot from the shore with long ropes attached to stern and bow or to the forward and rear thwarts (lining down). Very careful scouting of the steep plunge is required for rafts and decked canoes. The portage route around the plunge is on the left side of the river, and the route is fairly level and short, less than a 300-yard carry.

The drop is really more of an extreme slide, with a descent of about 6 feet over an 8-foot distance. The power of the turbulence below, where the raging forces of upthrust, side-eddies, and the main current crash together in utter chaos, is a sobering sight. While not impassable, it is a tough and dangerous spot.

There is nothing cute or tricky about maneuvering this chute, since there is no other place to go than right into its teeth. The biggest challenge is in not knifing so deeply into the massive curling combers and reverses below that you get smothered by the sheer force of the onrushing current. A spill right at the base, as the side currents slam into either side of the boat, could pitch the unwary into waters that could pin down even the strongest of swimmers.

From there on to Happy Camp is a treasure trove of isolated canyon, with enough rapids of modest caliber—nothing more than Class III—to add to the excitement and pleasure. One of the white-water stretches is in mid-canyon, just beyond the floating dock and boathouse where fishing guide Jim Rhoads beaches his jetboat and wooden river boats. The passage is purely a matter of high waves, and the worst of them can be bypassed on the left side. Downstream 4½ miles is the only other big water, where the current forks around a small gravel island. Coming out of the left fork, the combers are big, and open canoes may have to slice toward the right or lee side of the island to miss the worst.

Happy Camp to Salmon River
(*46 miles* • CLASS III–VI • *Running Time 15 hours*)
USGS 15 minute quadrangle maps
"Ukonom Lake," "Dillon Mtn.," and *"Forks of Salmon"*

• Little attention will be given to this stretch since it is definitely not recommended for open canoes or holiday boaters. Most of this run is through a deep canyon, with little or no access for takeouts should trouble develop. And there are enough difficult drops and chutes to cause trouble too, even for advanced paddlers.

The last obstacle is the worst—Ishi Pishi Falls, just out of Somesbar. It is an impassable series of 100-yard-long sloping boulder fields over which the river tumbles and plummets. There are some perpendicular 5- and 6-foot drops as well. (If you are in this area during the fall, you should make a point of stopping to watch the Klamath River Indians continue their traditional netting of the mighty fish negotiating the falls.)

Peaceful sweep of the Klamath near Happy Camp
is framed by a stream of reflected sunlight burning
through the smoke plume of a big lumber mill.
From Happy Camp to Ishi Pishi Falls, above
Orleans, is the only part of the river not suited to
open canoes. It is, however, a fine section of white
water for kayaks and rafters.

While Highway 96 offers a good vantage point for scouting the waters far below in the canyon, the depth of the canyon makes gauging the actual conditions difficult, at best. And it is tough, potentially dangerous water. Still, there are shorter segments closer to the road and nearer to Happy Camp that can be handled by top boaters after thorough car scouting.

The toughest and fastest water is along Buzzard Hill run, from Kanaka Creek to the Division of Highways maintenance station at U-Fish Creek. Another steep gradient, sometimes beyond 100 feet per mile, is from Independence Creek bridge to Swillup Creek, several miles above Blue Nose Bluff campgrounds.

Salmon River to Weitchpec
(*28 miles* • CLASS II–IV • *Running Time 9½ hours*)
USGS 15 minute quadrangle maps *"Orleans"* and *"Hoopa"*

• The rating here can be misleading, for this is a stretch that is easily conducive to open canoes manned by experienced fast-water paddlers. For the most part, the course here is a combination of deep quiet pools—strictly Class I—and short coursing chutes that reach up to Class IV. While the IVs have to be portaged, none of the carries is very long or arduous. For decked craft and rafts, this may be one of the finest runs on the river.

The best access, and a nice combination for an overnight run, is to put in from the Salmon River, just east of Somesbar, 6.2 miles up the Forks of the Salmon Road from Highway 96. The Salmon River provides the only boat access to this stretch of the Klamath, and the beginning riffles, chutes, and rapids of the smaller Salmon is an ideal spot to try out all hands before hitting bigger water. The access and the short Salmon River portion of this run are described in detail under the Salmon River section later in this book.

From the mouth of the Salmon, which can't be reached by car, the Klamath twists back and forth through a steep gorge, almost half a mile below the highway. The first mile from the confluence of the rivers is Class I water. Then a double chute demands a left of center course, quartering sharply through the first chute to miss heavy water on the right and a big rock on the left. The river then makes a sharp left S turn into the steep

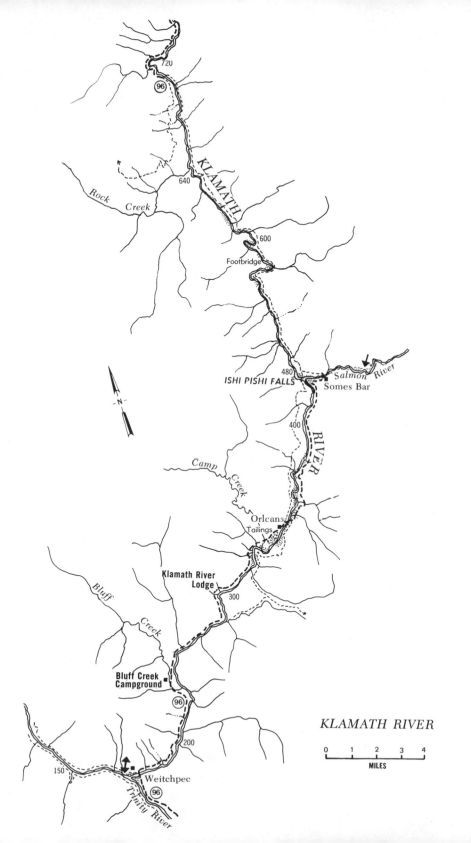

720

96

KLAMATH

640

Rock Creek

600

Footbridge

480
ISHI PISHI FALLS
Salmon River
Somes Bar

400

RIVER

Camp Creek

Orleans
Tailings

Klamath River Lodge

300

Bluff

Creek

Bluff Creek Campground

96

200

150
Weitchpec

96

Trinity River

KLAMATH RIVER

0 1 2 3 4
MILES

gorge. Coming out of the bottom of the S, there is a short but tough high-water chute, flanked by angled rock banks. The chute can be lined or portaged behind the rocks on the fairly level ground at the left bank.

The next half mile is flat water again, followed by another Class III drop with an easy portage on the right. Right below it, another 150 yards, is another steep drop, about a class tougher and much longer. The course is fairly straight and narrow, but the high waves and deep curls demand a portage for open canoes of about a quarter mile along the right bank.

Once past this stretch of white water, the gradient slows noticeably and Class I-II conditions prevail almost all the way to Weitchpec and the confluence of the Klamath with the Trinity. This section, and my family's problems on it, are described, of course, in the opening chapter of the book. Actually, the river deceived us in that maiden voyage. The box canyon below the Klamath River Lodge is rather foreboding; and half a mile below the lodge, the river hooks around a vertical cliff to the right and goes completely out of sight. It looks for all the world like it drops into a seething rapids—which is why we pulled out here after losing one of our paddles and much of our self-confidence during a thorough dunking. However, the river is in reality mostly smooth in this stretch, despite some treacherous looking undercurrents.

It is only another mile or two to Bluff Creek Forest Service campground. The landmark here is a huge pile of driftwood stacked by the current on the right-hand shore of a high gravel ledge, flanked by bedrock cliffs. This is where Bluff Creek joins in from the right. Back a few hundred yards from the river at this point, along the right side of the hill, there are a number of fine rough campsites, with fire grates, chemical toilets, and water. This spot makes an ideal overnight stop before resuming the remaining 10-mile jaunt to Weitchpec the following day.

This final lap, before hitting the confluence of the Klamath with the Trinity, is a continuation of mostly mild Class I-II conditions. The river attains greater size here and slows its descent noticeably. Even so, the current still makes a comfortable 4-5 miles an hour for the benefit of the lazy paddler.

The take-out is the same as for the end of the Trinity run, from the base of a long gravel bar just downstream of the Highway

96 bridge to Weitchpec. Only four-wheel-drive vehicles can make it down to the bank. Less fortunate souls must make a rather rigorous climb up the sandy bank to the roadbed. In doing so, they pass near a newly built ceremonial Indian dancing pit. Permission should be obtained from the owners there to both drive in and park your car.

Weitchpec to Pacific Ocean
(50 miles • CLASS I–II • *Running Time 15 hours)*
USGS 15 minute quadrangle maps
"Coyote Peak," "Tectah Creek," and "Klamath"

• Here, where the Trinity tumbles in from the south shore, the Klamath changes character most dramatically. From this confluence to its mouth at Requa on the Pacific, it is a broad, powerful, and mostly Class I river. There are few runs in the state that are more ideal for the beginning canoeist, although this should not be used as a first experience with current. The basic strokes and maneuvers must have been tested on a smaller, more tranquil river like the Russian. (Camping here also requires some previous experience.)

The current here is strong, running about 6 miles an hour most of the good boating year. Even casual boaters can easily make 25 miles a day. In late summer or early fall, however, water levels can drop, demanding more caution at rapids. The only obstacles to a complete Class I rating on this run are between the juncture of the two rivers and Pecwan Ridge, which is below the settlement of Johnsons on the deadend river road. Along this stretch, there are some chutes rated as Class II only because of the size of the combers and waves. There is plenty of room to draw clear of the roughest water.

The forested slopes of the canyon provide a wondrous backdrop to this scenic river valley, and you are at eye level with a wide variety of river life. Playful otters skittering along mud slides, setting up shop conveniently near the eddy pockets where Indians string their nets to trap unwary Chinook salmon heading upriver to spawn. Sleek mule deer mince deftly down steep banks to nibble tender sprouts and limbs, pausing now and then to bat their ears and flick their warning-flag tails in nervous gestures. Silent canoes are accepted as part of this natural domain and photographers can get some marvelous close-up shots at the water's edge.

From the access at Weitchpec to Johnsons is an easy one-day's run. Be sure to launch at the lower end of the gravel bar to miss the huge rapids just below where the Trinity comes in. Another hazard that must be watched for is the old Martin's Ferry bridge, washed out in the catastrophic flood of 1964. Jagged long struts from its superstructure still jut out into the water, just downstream from the new high-level bridge 6 miles below Weitchpec. It is about an hour's paddling time, or a bit less. The right side of the river gives easy and safe passage around the rusting relic. Then it's clear paddling, or coasting, to the ocean.

Ideal camping sites abound along this route. Tectah Creek is the first tributary of any size, coming in from the left about 5 or 6 miles below Johnsons, which can easily be spotted from the river by the cluster of homes and a large Indian church on the right. At Tectah, the creek has built a comfortable sand bar from winter storms and a clump of willows now offers ideal shelter for an overnight camp.

Another ideal campsite, to make an easy second day, is Blue Creek. The largest of the tributaries below the Trinity, its azure-hued waters sweep into the Klamath from the right about 10 miles below Tectah. Like Tectah, this is a popular salmon and steelhead spot, with fine trout fishing farther up the creek. The fish hole up in the scoured-out storm holes at the creek mouth, waiting for winter rains to start them on their spawning runs. Overland, the huge gravel bar at Blue Creek can be reached over a logging road along the Starwein Ridge leading out of Klamath Glen. However, permission to pass is needed from Simpson Lumber Company.

The downriver run from here on is uneventful. Cabins are more common, some reached by old logging roads, others only by boat. The mountain slopes dip closer and closer to the riverbed and are denuded of their forests. The best take-out, to avoid the flat slow water and stiff afternoon upriver winds from here to the mouth, is at the huge new levee built by the Army Corps of Engineers to keep the flood waters out of the Turwur Valley.

Other take-outs, should someone prefer going all the way to the inlet near the ocean mouth, are at any of a number of trail-

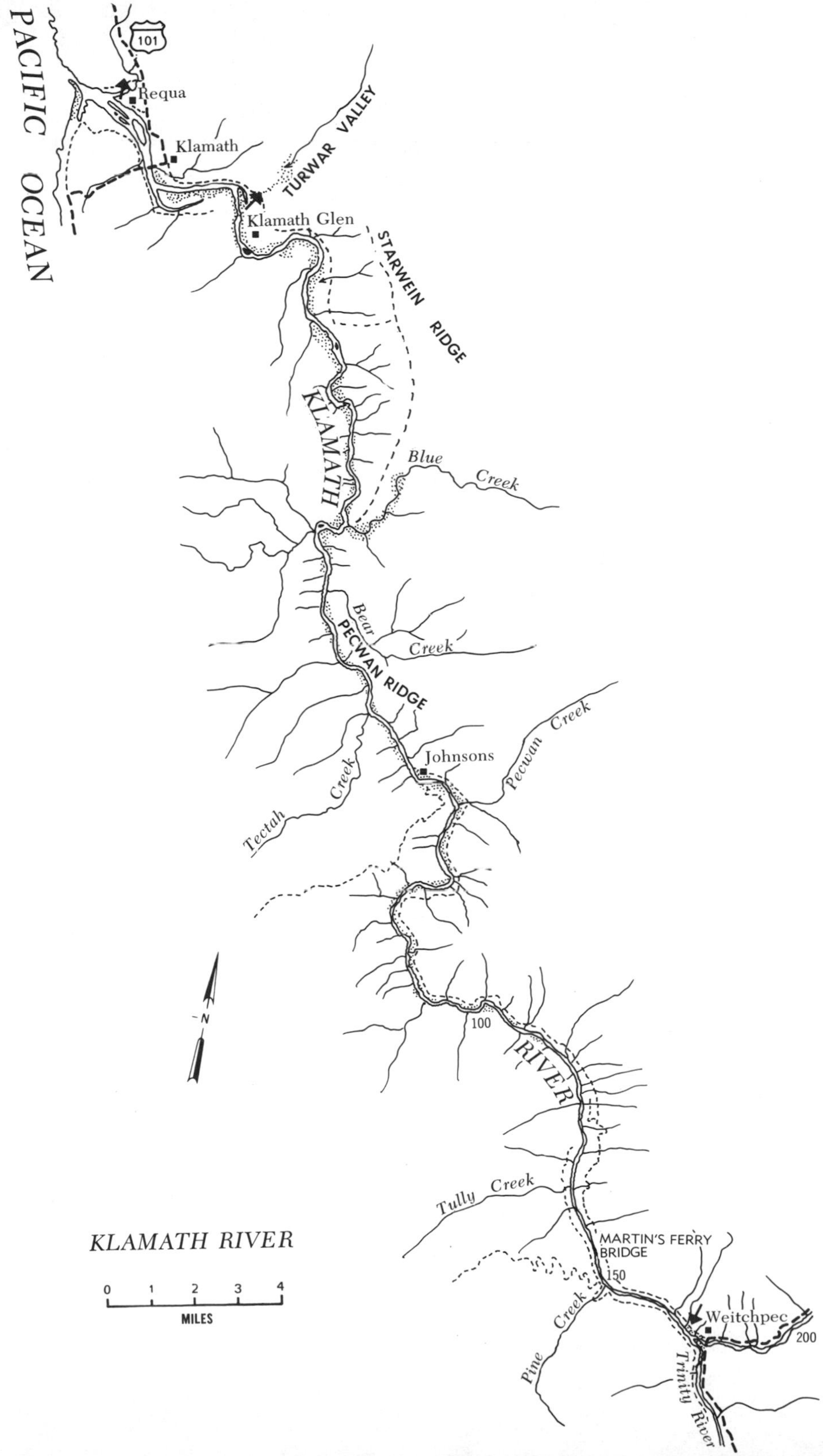

PACIFIC OCEAN

101

Requa

Klamath

TURWAR VALLEY

Klamath Glen

STARWEIN RIDGE

KLAMATH

Blue Creek

Bear Creek

PECWAN RIDGE

Tectah Creek

Johnsons

Pecwan Creek

N

100

RIVER

Tully Creek

MARTIN'S FERRY
BRIDGE

150

Pine Creek

Weitchpec

200

Trinity River

KLAMATH RIVER

0   1   2   3   4
MILES

er-park boat docks, for a small charge, or at a similar spot beneath the classic old hotel overlooking the bay at Requa another mile and a half toward the ocean.

One final note of caution about the Klamath. Like any river, the conditions depend upon the time of year. What is a placid Class I in early July, when we ran from Weitchpec, can turn into a raging hell during the mid-winter and early spring floods. Or it can become a tricky Class II–III in late August or September when the water drops very low and rapids develop between deep holding pools and shallow rocky stretches. A classic example of this kind of summertime drop is at Bear Creek Pools, about 6 miles below Pecwan bar, where a fast-moving riffle is broken with underwater rocks of some size. These are tricky but seldom dangerous. Moreover, the river is wide enough that boats can be walked or lined down along the edge should the passage become too shallow or otherwise too demanding. Never should a full portage be necessary.

In season, the Klamath offers an alternative method of shuttling from Klamath or Requa back to Weitchpec. You can board the sleek tourist jet boats for a one-way trip all the way back upriver to Johnsons, and beyond.

The Trinity River
(*98 miles* • CLASS I–VI)

THE past has robbed this once-brilliant ribbon of jeweled water of much of its virgin beauty. After more than a century of dreams—now properly recognized for what they really were, nightmares—civil engineers finally succeeded in turning the flow of this crystalline river eastward into the Sacramento. The goal was to quench the growing thirst of the burgeoning population "downstate," and the result was the near ruination of a great river system. There is now not enough sustained flow in the river to flush out the layers of silt that accumulate each winter from the lumbered watershed. As a result, summer water temperatures on the upper Trinity now consistently rise into the 70s, a most unhealthy situation for the river's trout or salmon.

And yet, there is hope. The Trinity is a hard loser and somehow retains enough of its magnetism to rank still as one of the best canoe runs in the state. If the current campaign to put the Trinity into a "wild and scenic river" designation succeeds, at least no more killer dams can deface it and despoil its remaining wilderness beauty. Meanwhile, despite the insults that man has heaped upon it, the Trinity has a great deal to offer. Snuggled between the searing heat of the Central Valley and the cool dampness of the coast, its climate is a study in comfortable moderation. It is 150 miles long from its headwaters in the Salmon and Scott Mountains to its confluence with the Klamath, although this guide deals only with the runs below Lewiston Dam. The dominant factor of its 3,000 square-mile watershed is the Trinity Alps, whose rugged granite slopes, sharp ridges, and serrated peaks closely resemble the Swiss mountains for which they were named. It also is steeped in the history of its rambunctious past, when every riffle and gravel bar was crowded with wild-eyed 49ers, panning for a quick fortune in gold nuggets.

Lewiston to Helena
(*32 miles* • CLASS I–II • *Running Time 9 hours*)
USGS 15 minute quadrangle maps
"Weaverville," "Hayfork," and "Helena"

• This upper stretch of the river below Clair Engle Lake and Lewiston Dam is an ideal piece of water for open canoes and other craft, except during periods of low water. As elsewhere in the state, the diverters and power people have wreaked their usual havoc on the navigable rivers. Anytime after early July, the first 9-mile stretch to Douglas City is likely to feature at least half a dozen small rocky rapids that must be walked because of low water.

This upper run is primarily a Class II, with one or two Class III stretches, depending upon the water flow. The put-in for the upper run is from a bar near the gauging station below Lewiston, leaving Highway 299 at the Lewiston turnoff, which is about 40 miles west of Redding. The initial 5 miles on the river has a gentle gradient and is uneventful, but then the Trinity makes one of the most unusual maneuvers among the state's rivers.

The toe of the Brown Mountains is the obstacle and the Trinity careens into an exaggerated boot-shaped turn to get around it. Beyond where the current slams into the mountains and bends sharply to the right, heading for the "toe," there are two small cabins up the left bank. The rapids here are not too tough to negotiate on the right side of the bend.

There is another small cabin on the bank of Limekiln Gulch on the right, which marks the toe and a sharp left turn heading down the "sole" of the "boot." The river then makes a slight jog left at the "instep" and bends very sharply in a nearly complete 180-degree left-hand turn around the "heel." A small cluster of summer homes are along the left bank coming out of the "heel," and from there the river picks up a bit of steam as it straightens out for about a mile before bending back to the right again to Douglas City.

For those who want to bypass this isolated stretch, they can launch from a swimming beach at a Bureau of Land Management campground downstream from Douglas City, along the river road on the east side of the river. Douglas City is also a good overnight

Inflatable kayak bounces over the lip of a sharp
drop on the upper Trinity River downstream of
Lewiston Dam. Much of the river's course, though
paralleled by Highway 299, is isolated by a wall of
heavy vegetation. The Trinity is the longest and
best mountain stream canoe water in the state,
especially for family sport in summer.

stop, since the BLM campground has a big swimming hole and many rough campsites.

The 15-mile run on to Junction City carries a slightly bigger head of water. thanks to Weaver Creek that enters just below Douglas City.

There are also several exciting Class II runs between Douglas and Steiner Flat as Highway 299 arcs away from the river through a canyon. A rock and sand bar on the left side at Steiner's Flat, where two homes can be seen far up the flat on the right side, was our campsite on this run. There are only a limited number of good campsites from here down to Junction City, but enough to suffice.

The next stretch is comparatively easy, as the river flattens out. Some runs may have to be forded because of low water. One such spot is where the river makes a graduated, inverted V-turn to the right. Another and much sharper V-turn is in the opposite direction a mile further on, just below Maxwell Creek, which comes in on the left.

The remainder of the run to Junction City is marked by gold tailings piled on the north bank, silted holes lined with cattails, and a slow pace. There is ideal take-out access just below the Junction City bridge on the right bank.

A continuation to Helena picks up faster water with the addition of the largest tributary on this stretch, Clear Creek. The rapids are quick and bouncy and the water deep enough to give clearance from the boulders below. This 9-mile run may be the best part of the Lewiston–Helena route. In the summer, it also offers some fairly good angling for planted trout; and in the fall, with its lower water temperatures, there is good fishing for salmon.

The ideal take-out and camping access on this run is at the Pigeon Point campground, less than half a mile downstream from Helena. It is on the right bank just after the combined North and East Forks of the Trinity come dashing in on the right side.

The splendid isolation of the Trinity Gorge
between Hoopa Valley and Weitchpec frames
these paddlers. Snaking through an isolated
canyon, the river is flat and smooth for nearly 8
miles between vertical rock walls.

Helena to Cedar Flat Campground
(*25 miles* • CLASS III–V)
USGS 15 minute quadrangle maps
"Helena," "Hayfork," and "Ironside Mtn."

• This area is definitely not recommended for open boats. Highway 299 parallels the river most of the way and a car scout will quickly reveal the reasons why. Best in the late spring and early summer, the first 12 miles, from Pigeon Point to Big Bar, could be handled by intermediate canoeists, through a series of Class II–III drops. There are at least two rapids here, however, that would have to be upgraded a class in heavier spring water and would require a short portage by open craft. For decked boats, it might be an ideal one-day run. The last half of the run gets more severe, with some powerful rapids and chutes.

Cedar Flat, just downstream of the Highway 299 bridge that puts the road on the left side of the river, is the deadend of this segment, literally speaking. The Trinity turns away from the highway here, plunging down a steep, vertical-walled canyon. Less than 3 miles into this cauldron is Burnt Ranch Falls, a succession of steep drops, wildly high waves, and massive boulders that make it impassable. Two miles further down—and I do mean *down*—is another treacherous piece of water, Gray Falls, which offers more of the same.

Hawkins Bar to Willow Creek
(*16 miles* • CLASS I–III • *Running Time 5½ hours*)
USGS 15 minute quadrangle map *"Willow Creek"*

• The first 4 miles of this run are the toughest. The river, falling away at between 20 and 40 feet per mile, loops away from 299 and then back again 3 miles above Salyer Station. The Class III water is limited to this brief area; and while it is exciting for boaters of intermediate caliber, it can be bypassed by beginners by putting in above Salyer where the river sweeps back toward the highway. The carry from the Highway 299 side is fairly steep. A better put-in site is on the other side of the river, reached by turning north across the river at Salyer and taking the river frontage road to the right on the other side of the high and rickety one-way bridge. There is a turnout down to the river

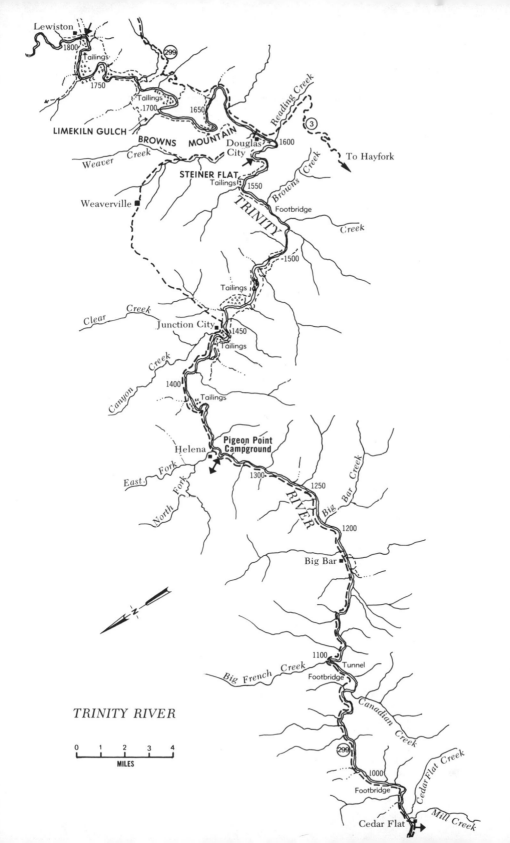

Lewiston
1800
Tailings
1750
Tailings
1700
1650
LIMEKILN GULCH
BROWNS MOUNTAIN
Weaver Creek
Douglas City
299
3
1600
Reading Creek
To Hayfork
STEINER FLAT
Tailings
1550
Browns Creek
TRINITY
Weaverville
Footbridge
Creek
1500
Tailings
Clear Creek
Junction City
1450
Tailings
Canyon Creek
1400
Tailings
Pigeon Point
Campground
Helena
East Fork
North Fork
1300
1250
Big Bar Creek
RIVER
1200
Big Bar
1100
Tunnel
Big French Creek
Footbridge
Canadian Creek
299
1000
Footbridge
Cedar Flat Creek
Mill Creek
Cedar Flat

TRINITY RIVER

0 1 2 3 4
MILES

3 miles along this road, at the bottom of a sloping hill, and the boats can be launched in a quiet pool.

The remainder of the run is a classic stretch of Class I–II water, sprinkled with only modest rapids and several riffles. Ideal swimming holes abound in this deep canyon run and the summer-time temperatures—both in the air and water—are conducive to some of the most pleasant river swimming in the state. If taken late in the summer, a few of the shallower riffles on this run might have to be walked.

The South Fork of the Trinity comes in 2 miles below Salyer and another 3 miles downstream is the only exception to the river's mild nature. The river flattens out along a wide gravel bar for several hundred yards, but a pronounced dip in the land-scape at the end of the bar signals fast water. This quick chute is pocked with sharp sub-surface rocks, demanding a quick slalom maneuver at its upper lip. It then careens into an exaggerated left turn at full speed near the base of the run. A great piece of water for decked crafts and small rafts, this section should be bypassed by all but expert open-canoe hands. The bypass is through some small walk-through channels on the far left side of the river, beginning in the lower end of the big pool. The river returns to a constant Class I–II thereafter, all the way to the Trinity Gorge on the next full run.

Willow Creek to Weitchpec
(17 miles • CLASS II–III • Running Time 7 hours)
USGS 15 minute quadrangle maps
"Willow Creek" and "Hoopa"

• I rate this entire Salyer–Weitchpec section as among the best in the state for open canoes. It is pleasant and exciting but not dangerous, and the scenery is unsurpassed. It is a must for the type of family canoeing that inspired this book. To get access to the Trinity from Willow Creek, turn north off 299 one block east of the Highway 96 junction which leads to the fairgrounds. Just beyond, bear to the left down past a ball field to a gravel bar and the river.

The Trinity winds through three separate gorges on this stretch, each of them beautiful, isolated, and completely safe. The first begins just a few miles downstream from the put-in

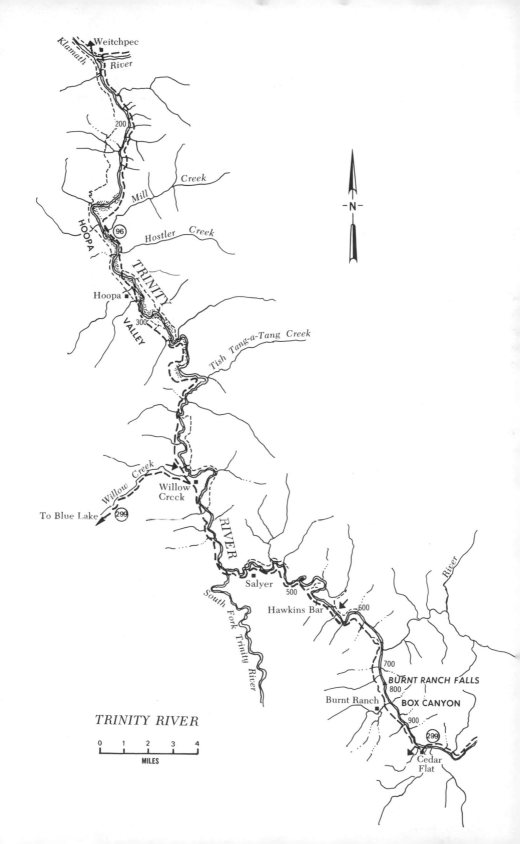

TRINITY RIVER

0   1   2   3   4
MILES

and is sprinkled with an exciting series of bumpy Class II chutes that offer no severe challenges. There are beautiful sand bar campsites, ringed by high rocky cliffs. The deep holes are favorite holding spots for big salmon and steelhead, though it takes great patience and a fine fly-fishing routine to put much of any size into the creel before the half-pounders start moving in August or September.

The first trouble of any kind comes about 6 miles into the first gorge. A beautiful summer home overlooks the gorge high on the left cliffs. A quarter of a mile downstream, the river forks slightly at a moderate chute. The left side of the left fork provides safe if somewhat bumpy passage around sub-surface rocks and high combers.

Beyond this spot, there is nothing requiring scouting reports until a big highway construction slide on the left bank, several miles downstream. Half a mile downstream from that site, the Trinity powers head-on into a massive rocky cliff, creating a huge back-boil on the right and slightly downstream side. The current is so swift here that you must stay exactly on the right-hand edge, just distant enough to miss being swept into the cliff on the sharp turn but near enough to keep the bow from getting caught in the strong reverse sweep. If you can't pull free of the boil, then merely crouch low in the boat and keep your balance. The subsequent spin won't be wholly unpleasant, and it is better to ride it out than to fight a losing battle.

It is 10 miles through the Hoopa Valley until the next gorge, and much of this stretch is flat water, marked by strong upriver winds in the afternoon. The few rapids are desirable interludes to the torturous rhythm of paddling, and several of them are flanked by bushes loaded with succulent blackberries.

This second gorge is also the prettiest on the river. The sheer rock walls frame the flat moving current and the 15-20-foot deep holes over which it gracefully slides. Here, in the cool shelter of the deep water, in shadow from the cliffs for all but a few hours of the day, salmon and steelhead wait for the cooling fall rains before resuming their upstream migration. In season, anglers should break out their gear for some of the finest drift fishing on the river. The key to success here is to put the lure or bait near to the bottom where the customers are.

Turbulent Class IV rapid near the end of the
Lower Trinity Gorge tosses rubber kayak over
massive combers like a drifting leaf. It is the only
impassable spot on the lower river for open
canoes.

The canyon widens, almost imperceptibly, 4 miles into the gorge. There are no rapids or obstacles worthy of mention. The first and most difficult hurdle comes about a mile beyond the gorge. When the river swings right and a creek cascades down a jagged rock slide on the right, the approach to a river-wide falls is about an eighth of a mile downstream. The sound and tumult of the rushing water at this point should be warning enough.

The term "falls" is somewhat misleading. Actually, it is a river-wide boulder field through which the water tumbles down a short, steep gradient. Only the far right side of this drop can be safely handled; the rest of it is pocked with sharp underwater rocks. Since this spot is also the first really suitable campsite area beyond the entire Hoopa Valley and its second gorge, a pull-out is appropriate anyway. The campsite is on the left bank, the take-out just a few yards above the brink of the falls.

The next mile or two beyond this sweep is faster water but mostly uneventful. Rounding a right turn, the roar of white water signals the time for another scouting foray through an obvious boulder field. At this point, the Weitchpec Store is visible straight ahead, a mile downstream and high above the river. These rapids ought to be portaged by open canoes, and the left side offers the best footing for a short 70-yard haul.

At the mouth of the Trinity, the path leading up to Weitchpec is tortuous for packing gear and canoes. One trip with the deflated kayak prompted us to line the Starcraft 300 yards up the Klamath, which gave us enough room to sweep across the river above the swiftest part of the current and before it piles into heavy Class III–IV rapids. Then, it was a long carry up the sand bar to the bench above where our shuttle car waited.

A last word on the Trinity. It is not essential to make a take-out by lining up the Klamath, nor even to make a take-out at all. From Weitchpec to the ocean, the Klamath offers some excellent boating and fishing, as I noted. If you should continue into the Klamath, lean into your paddling with a vengeance to draw fully across the swift powerful current and to avoid being swept into the rapids that skirt the left side of the river. There is sufficient room to draw clear on the right of the high combers and deep troughs, but only after some very exercised paddling.

The Eel River
(*204 miles* • CLASS I–IV)

No other river with a watershed entirely within the boundaries of the Golden State yields as much water as the mighty Eel. Nor is it likely that any other river has as many diverse flow patterns. Draining a 3,565-square-mile area spread over four counties, the Eel dumps about 6 million acre-feet of water a year into the Pacific, 13 miles south of Eureka. Because the river's denuded watershed is no longer able to soak up the torrential rain storms that are the river's main source, the Eel also carries a fantastic silt load to sea in the winter and early spring floods and has recently gained the reputation for being one of the dirtiest streams on the continent. On the other hand, the rambunctious winter and spring activity of the river leaves a scant 1 percent of its flow for the summer months, from July through October.

So, you see, it's either feast or famine on the Eel. Spring is almost too soon to ply its waters—July, too late. And after July, there are stretches that wouldn't float a balsa log. (The Main Eel's loss becomes the Russian River's gain at Lake Pillsbury, where much of the flow is sucked off for shipment down the Russian to the fertile vineyards below.)

Still, at the right season, the three main branches—the Main Eel and its Middle and South Forks—offer a wonderful variety along 226 miles of streambed, most of them suitable for open canoes. Furthermore, the majority of those miles are through some of the state's most beautiful rolling countryside, much of it semi-wilderness where the outside world seldom makes an inroad. Through May and June, there are few rivers in the nation that offer such rich rewards, and commercial rafts, kayaks, canoes, even air mattresses and inner tubes ride its watery trails. River safaris at this time of year, when the Eel has on its most vibrantly scenic face, make it difficult to believe the force and ugliness of the roily winter flood waters. In late spring, only a slightly opaque, milky tint remains of the sediment of winter.

One of the few major river systems on the continent that flow northward, the Eel became the center of controversy in the late 1960s, when sportsmen and conservationists joined hands to defeat plans for a high dam at Dos Rios that would have flooded the incomparably beautiful Round Valley. The dam would also have wiped out one of the finest canoe runs in the north end of the state, along the Middle Fork of the Eel from Black Butte River to Dos Rios. Of course, water companies and lumbering interests still have a strong vested interest in harnessing the river system in the name of flood control. Even while this book was being penned, the Eel was again part of a controversial struggle—this one to designate and preserve it as a wild and scenic river, along with its two wild brothers, the Klamath and Trinity. If that struggle is still going on as you are reading this, and if you have any hopes of ever boating along this marvelous river, you would do well to roll up your sleeves and take up the cause before it is too late.

THE MAIN EEL
(*142 miles* • CLASS I–IV)

Lake Pillsbury to Van Arsdale Reservoir
(*10 miles* • CLASS III–IV • *Running Time 3½ hours*)
USGS 15 minute quadrangle maps
"Lake Pillsbury" and "Potter Valley"

• This isolated upper-canyon run is one of the most beautiful on the entire river. Unfortunately, despite the breathtaking scenery, the riverbed is a jagged obstacle course of upthrust boulders, except at high water levels. It is just too precipitous and rocky for open canoes, but it is ideal water for good hands in decked canoes, kayaks, and small rafts.

Access to this run is reached by turning east off Highway 101 at Calpella, north of Ukiah, onto State Route 20. Seven miles along Highway 20, turn left (north) on the Potter Valley Road, following it all the way through Potter Valley to the F.M. Crawford sawmill. Turn right there and follow the frontage road on the south side of Van Arsdale until you reach the end of slack water. That is the take-out. Launch from just below Scott Dam, on Lake Pillsbury, 10 miles upstream at the first or second bridge crossing.

The North Fork of the Eel River.

Hearst to Outlet Creek
(18 miles · CLASS II–III · Running Time 7½ hours)
USGS 15 minute quadrangle maps
"Eden Valley" and "Laytonville"

• The put-in for this stretch at Hearst is reached from the Longvale-Dos Rios Road. As with much of the Eel, the run is usable only in spring months. The gradient is fairly pronounced in short pieces of this streambed, producing some challenging Class III rapids that for open canoes demand considerable skill in staying upright. It is a prized run for commercial rafts, kayaks, and white-water canoes.

The mileage of this run can be deceiving; for so much scouting of the water and rapids is usually required that the full run of 18 miles demands an overnight schedule. An overnight camp is hardly a penalty, however, considering the beauty of the wildlife and unusual geologic formations in the area.

Dos Rios to Alderpoint
(55 miles · CLASS II–III · Running Time 16 hours)
USGS 15 minute quadrangle maps
"Laytonville," "Spy Rock," "Kettenpom," and "Alderpoint"

• The descent of the river here doesn't change much from the upper run, but the addition of the Middle Fork of the river at Dos Rios more than doubles the flow. Only experienced boaters will be able to negotiate this challenging combination of pools, rapids, and drops. As in almost every major river channel, boaters should plan to make most of their distance in the morning hours. Strong upriver winds are common from about 1–5 P.M., bringing high waves and difficult paddling. The put-in access is from a long bar at the junction of the Main and Middle Forks. Turn off Highway 261 from Longvale to Covelo, either just before crossing the bridge over the Middle Fork or half a mile south to catch the lower part of the Main Fork.

Large groups of Sierra Club paddlers have made this an annual Memorial Day pilgrimage, and the colorful combination of kayaks, open and decked canoes, and rafts gives the river a carnival-like air for the three-day assault. During the earlier weeks of the spring, the attractions are all pleasantly obvious. The track

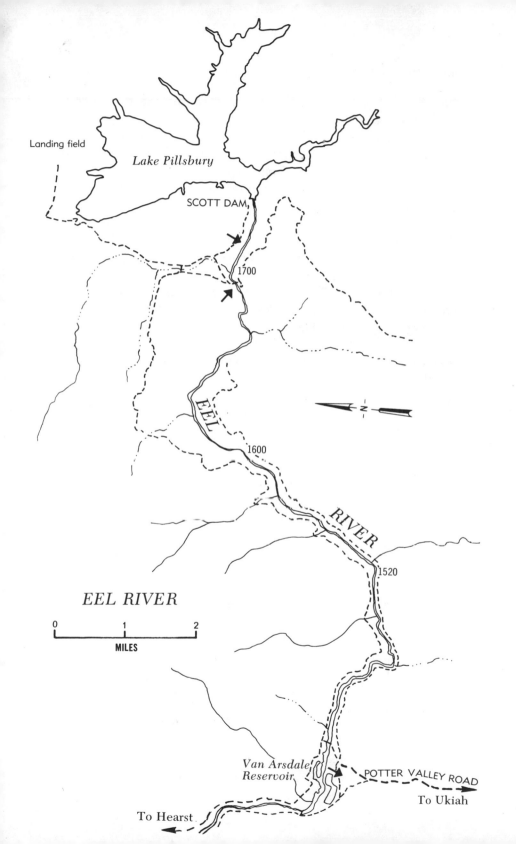

Landing field

Lake Pillsbury

SCOTT DAM

1700

EEL

1600

RIVER

1520

EEL RIVER

0   1   2
MILES

Van Arsdale
Reservoir

POTTER VALLEY ROAD

To Ukiah

To Hearst

bed of the Northwestern Pacific Railroad and the few isolated townsites it still serves are the only signs of civilization. Deer, the occasional bear and coyote, and even a few wild boars can be seen by the alert shore-watcher. While most of the heavy lumber has been stripped from the hills that flank the valley, the second growth brings a delightful emerald cast to the picturesque landscape.

Campsites along sand bars are too numerous to count, and most of them have an ample supply of driftwood for fires. The Alderpoint take-out is easily reached by road, although it is a fairly circuitous route from Dos Rios. Shuttle cars must take the Dos Rios–Laytonville cutoff to 101, a narrow gravel road reached by turning left (east) after crossing the Middle Fork bridge on the way to Covelo. Once back on 101, northbound, you head for Garberville, taking the second Garberville off-ramp, marked Redway. Turn left over the freeway at the top of the ramp, and half a mile further on, at the right, is the turn-off to Alderpoint. Drive right down to the center of the village, making a right turn on Main Street past the Alderpoint store. Then, head down to the river on the frontage road, and at the Alderpoint bridge bear to the right, upriver, for half a mile to a major logging station. Turn left into the storage yard, cross the tracks, and bear left again to the road down to the gravel bar.

Alderpoint to Fernbridge
(*88 miles* • CLASS I • *Running Time 40 hours*)
USGS 15 minute quadrangle maps
"Alderpoint," "Blocksburg," "Weott," "Scotia," "Fortuna"

• From the same Alderpoint access described above, boaters can embark on a 38-mile jaunt to South Fork. This is a peaceful stretch, perfect for beginners and worthwhile for more experienced paddlers seeking a comfortable change of pace. There is a seemingly endless horizon through this valley, with abandoned homesteads and logging camps that evoke its storied past. Such fanciful names as Mount Baldy, Billy Goat Peak, and Island and Chalk Mountains are just a sample of this region's colorful history and topography. Campsites abound on either bank all the way to South Fork, where the Main Eel joins with its South Fork to wend its way to the sea between ridges and through stately

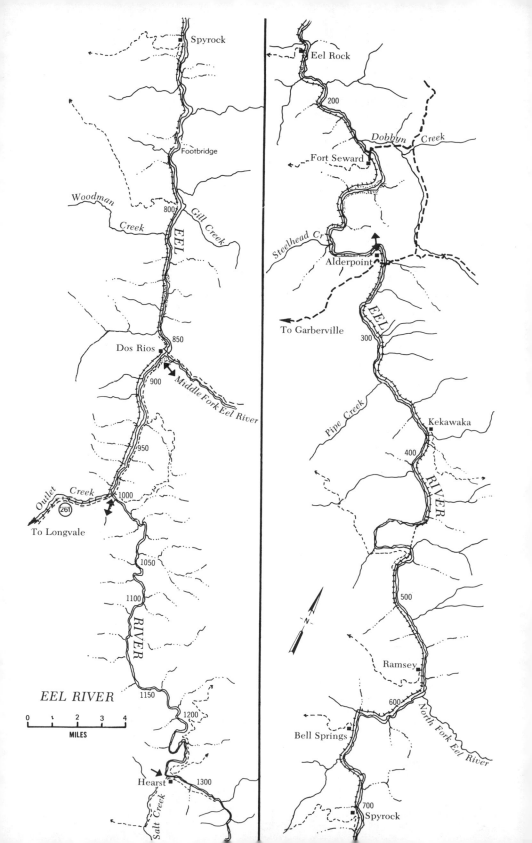

EEL RIVER

Spyrock

Footbridge

Woodman Creek

Gill Creek

EEL

800

850

Dos Rios

900

Middle Fork Eel River

950

Outlet Creek

1000

261

To Longvale

1050

1100

RIVER

1150

1200

EEL RIVER

0 1 2 3 4
MILES

Hearst

1300

Salt Creek

Eel Rock

200

Dobbyn Creek

Fort Seward

Steelhead Cr

Alderpoint

To Garberville

EEL

300

Pipe Creek

Kekawaka

400

RIVER

500

N

Ramsey

600

North Fork Eel River

Bell Springs

700

Spyrock

groves of redwoods. Unfortunately, the water level drops below the navigational limits in the late fall, when the whole sweeping panorama comes alive in a stunning kaleidoscope of autumn finery.

During the navigable months, the first 10-mile section—the S-loop from Alderpoint to Fort Seward—is the only rapids of sufficient difficulty to warrant description. Four miles south of Alderpoint, the first major right-hand curve appears and begins the S. In the middle of the half-mile long sweep, Steelhead Creek tumbles airily beneath the Northwestern Pacific trestle on the left shore. Just beyond, as the Eel swings back to the right at the top of the S, the river funnels down into a swift chute that is more deceptive than dangerous. However, caution is needed to skirt the high rollers that can splash in over the gunwhales.

The Eel flattens and slows considerably beneath the S-curve, and it remains much the same throughout the final two thirds of the journey to South Fork, although the scenery improves in the final 10 miles as you near the Stephenson's, Burlington, and Dyerville Flats redwood groves. The majesty of these forest giants alone makes the trip worthwhile, especially the magnificent specimen on North Dyerville Flat that reaches 364 feet toward the heavens that rain down its nourishment. It is said to be one of the world's tallest living trees.

The abandonment by Northwestern Pacific of the scenic "Skunk" steam-engine passenger service robs this run of access. At Fort Seward, there is a take-out on the left bank just upstream from the bridge connection with the road to Alderpoint. The only settlements below Fort Seward served by road are Sequoia, Devil's Elbow, McCann, and Camp Grant. The trip can be shortened by about 15 miles by taking out at Sequoia, an abandoned lumber town and the first highway access below Seward. The river here is just a quarter of a mile away from the road on the right side. The first bridge crossing is 5 miles further on, at McCann.

The scenery is a silent but powerful command to finish the lap at least to South Fork. From Dyerville, just a few miles beyond McCann, to the town of South Fork, where the branch bearing that name converges, the Eel turns into a quiet, peaceful, elongated pool. Redwoods rise majestically on either side, and while

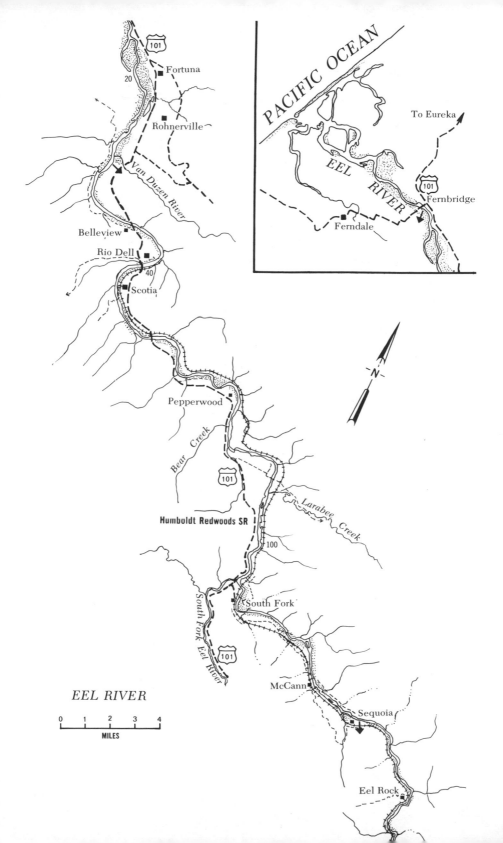

PACIFIC OCEAN

EEL RIVER

To Eureka

Fernbridge

Ferndale

Fortuna

Rohnerville

Van Duzen River

Belleview

Rio Dell

Scotia

Pepperwood

Bear Creek

Larabee Creek

Humboldt Redwoods SR

South Fork

South Fork Eel River

McCann

Sequoia

Eel Rock

EEL RIVER

0 1 2 3 4

MILES

a steady paddling rhythm is needed to finish the course, the miles seem to flash effortlessly by. The eternal nature of the mighty giants of the forest pale hours into the insignificant fragments of time they really are.

Boaters can trace the meandering Eel another 50 miles from South Fork all the way to its mouth, given the right tidal exchange. A more practical take-out, however, would be at the Ferndale–Fernbridge crossing 1½ miles from the tidal lagoon. And before it meets the Pacific, the river parallels the freeway almost all the way from Pepperwood and the border of the redwood forest, making take-outs a delightfully flexible matter. Another available take-out is at the wide bar where the Van Duzen River flows in from the right, just upstream of the Highway 36 bridge.

Throughout this whole section of the Eel in the pleasant spring months, another vibrant life cycle is enacted—the age-old annual migration upstream of the Lamprey eels. The slender but muscular aquatic serpents love basking in midstream, just inches beneath the surface, undulating their bodies for just enough headway to match the push of the current. We've been startled many times when our paddles brushed one of these sun-bathers and it rocketed off in a panic of spray and thrashing. Apparently, the layer upon layer of silt that has accumulated in the river bed is less hostile to the spawning process of eels than it is for the lessening number of steelhead and salmon that still swim and spawn in these waters.

THE MIDDLE FORK
(*31 miles* • CLASS II–V)

Black Butte River to Dos Rios
(*31 miles* • CLASS II–V • *Running Time 11 hours*)
USGS 15 minute quadrangle maps
"Covelo" and "Laytonville"

• The Black Butte River flows into the Middle Fork of the
Eel about 12.5 miles east of Covelo. To reach the put-in, take
county road 338 to the right at the junction, 1.5 miles from Covelo
and just beyond the forest ranger station. A sweeping gravel bar
200 yards above the confluence provides a good launching spot
for the vigorous and exciting 31-mile trip through some of the
finest wilderness and wild-river areas in the state.

The water level fluctuates dramatically from winter to summer on this area of the mighty 142-mile-long river. Not unexpec-
tedly, so does the classification system that tries to typify the
boating conditions. In May and early June, the run is an ideal
Class II, except for its final 9 miles with which we will deal
later. Conversely, the river is treacherously faster during the
flood run-out of winter and early spring. On our tour, we found
the twisted hulk of a battered aluminum canoe tangled in a rock
jam—grim testimony to the Eel's deceptive power when the
water runs high and wild.

During the navigable season, there are some exciting and
choppy Class II rapids and a swift 6-mile-per-hour current, but
almost every run offers safe, if wet, passage down the edge of
the white water. We took the more thrilling stretches but had
to pay for it by stopping every few miles to bail out the excess
water. The river snakes back and forth through a forested and
isolated canyon, its gradient a pleasant 20–25 feet to the mile
for the first 17–18 miles. It is separated from Round Valley by

a high ridge, and the boater sees nothing of civilization from the put-in point until he spots the wooden fence of the Levi Ranch far below on the following day.

Ideal camping sites proliferate along both banks, offering either protected sand bars in the lee of wind-breaking boulders or more scenic spots beneath the pines, giant oaks, and towering madrone trees that dot the hillsides. On our first night, we spotted deer, raccoon, quail, and signs of wild turkeys. Even bear are said to frequent the riverbanks here when the spawning runs are in full swing. Nothing but the sounds of nature breaks the utter and peaceful silence in this piece of the Middle Eel. This part of the Eel is also highly rated steelhead water in the summer, though not quite in the same class as the waters below Van Arsdale Reservoir on the main stem.

There are too many rapids along the middle portion of this run to describe each of them, and the landmarks are too difficult to define. But the average canoeist has nothing to fear, at least not until he passes the last major tributary, Elk Creek, which enters from the left, just in front of a beautiful grassy meadow at the water's edge. About 2 miles beyond Elk Creek are the first major rapids of the entire run. We found that the best take-out spot and scouting platform for the 150-yard run is on the left bank, near where a steep gravel bank rises about 10 feet above the water.

In making the run, you'll need to perform a series of slalom maneuvers in order to skirt underwater rocks heading into the white water. Then, in order to meet a demanding drop through a narrow boulder-flanked chute at the base of the rapids, you'll have to cut across current and reverse quickly as you slide up the crest of a big boil, arrowing sharply to the right. Then it is just a hell-for-leather race right across the face of the current toward the left side to clear some ominous rocks below. When you have completed this stretch, I guarantee that you'll pause in the mild chop below, breathless and electric with the excitement.

The Levi Ranch fencing, long wooden poles stretching across a meadow 200 yards above the right bank, is the landmark for a take-out to avoid the heavy water between here and Dos Rios. Access permission must be obtained from the owner beforehand, on the way from Dos Rios to the put-in at Covelo (specific direc-

Inflatable kayak bobs peacefully through the
isolated midsection of the Eel River's middle fork
behind Round Valley, a truly wilderness experience
for an overnight run. The 22-mile run from Black
Butte River to Levi Ranch is an ideal Class II-III
overnighter and one of the prime canoe runs in
the state.

tions can be obtained at the store in Dos Rios or at resort lodges between there and Covelo). Beyond the Levi Ranch, the scenery begins to change from rocky pine and oak country to chaparral. Then you will be upon the upper reaches of Ike's Gorge and Germain's rapids, as well as the final 9½ miles of the run.

There is virtually nothing to recommend this last stretch to anyone but white-water rats, except that the gorge is isolated and possessed of a rugged beauty. While the rapids are frequent and thrilling, with deep rollers, high frothy crests, and demanding turns, the passageway is also marked with at least four runs that demand back-breaking portages for canoe campers. The worst of the runs are spaced about 1½ miles apart, while the descent drops quickly from a modest gradient to nearly 75 feet per mile.

At least one of the runs is completely impassable, even for experts in kayaks and white-water canoes. The others are safe only for those experts. All of the runs are well marked by the roar of white water and the graphic drop of the ridge line just ahead. The first two are best negotiated by right-hand pullouts— the first at the top of the swift glide heading into the white water, and the second into a quiet pool on the far right, just in front of the rapids that curve away sharply to the left. The third rapids features an impassable, 4-foot high falls across all but the narrowest of chutes on the far left side. We walked our loaded 15-footer down the right-hand fork, shallow and studded with rocks, and lowered it over the lip of the drop into the frothy pool below.

The fourth and last obstacle, at the base of the gorge, is a massive, half-mile jumble of huge rocks, tumbled into the river from a major landslide on the steep left bank of the gorge. The portage here should be on the right bank; we tried the left, and after picking our way through huge boulders and under a fallen giant oak, we were finally blocked by a sharp cliff, with another third of the jagged boulder field still below us.

At that point, we had only one choice; mincing across the face of a steep slide, we angled down to the water and lashed in again just in time for the worst of the drops. Hugging the rocks and back-paddling strenuously for every additional second to scout the turbid, swirling water ahead, we found that the rest of the river was an impassable 5-foot-high falls and that the only opening on the left broke wildly between two outcroppings.

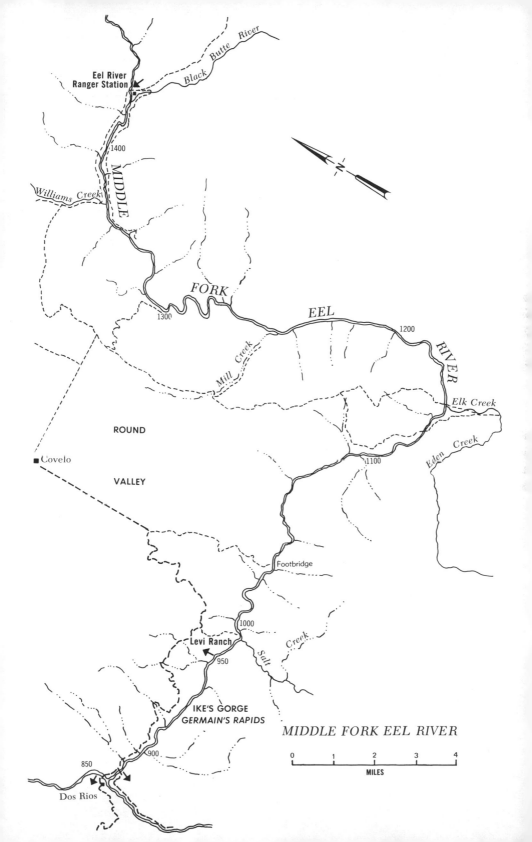

Eel River
Ranger Station

Black Butte River

1400

MIDDLE

Williams Creek

FORK

1300

EEL

1200

RIVER

Mill Creek

Elk Creek

Eden Creek

ROUND

1100

■ Covelo

VALLEY

Footbridge

1000

Salt Creek

Levi Ranch

950

IKE'S GORGE
GERMAIN'S RAPIDS

900

MIDDLE FORK EEL RIVER

850

Dos Rios

0   1   2   3   4
MILES

We had to dip into the chute as the current swept us up the face of a large boil pushed up by rocks below. Vance's artfully timed backstroke on the left side of the stern, and my strong sweep on the starboard bow, took the prow past the jagged rock on the right side of the slide. Then, a quick reverse slid us up the crest of the boil and down into a right-angle slick, where left drawstrokes on the bow prevented a broadside slip. We both hung limp as the canoe swirled slowly around in the pool below, gliding quietly downstream. Here had been another demanding test of our skill. A split second mistake either way, a moment's hesitation, and we would have taken a nasty spill.

There are three more stiff Class II rapids in the next 2 miles; but while we took some heavy spray from the pounding chop, it was a cakewalk compared to the obstacle we had just passed. The best take-out and access is on the left side of the Longvale–Covelo road bridge. The second access, just beyond at Dos Rios, is much steeper.

The final 9½ miles had taken us at least four hours to run, counting the many portages and scouting forays we had to make as we cased hidden waters beyond short turns in the gorge. I would rate the upper 22 miles as a beautiful Class II. In the few places where the waves are high enough to break over the bow, there is usually sufficient room to draw clear in less bumpy water. A spraydeck would be helpful, however, and save considerable bailing time. The last 9½ miles, however, are closer to a consistent Class III, with the last of the four main rapids rating Class V and the third, impassable. The run, of course, is much easier for kayaks and decked canoes. It is also a popular commercial rafting trip during the higher water of early spring.

THE SOUTH FORK
(*84 miles* • CLASS I–IV)

Branscomb to The Hermitage
(*18 miles* • CLASS III–IV • *Running Time 6½ hours*)
USGS 15 minute quadrangle map
"Branscomb" and "Leggett"

• The South Fork of the Eel snakes through some of the coastal range's most scenic and protected wilderness. After swelling from a profusion of creeks at its headwaters, just north of the Willits–Fort Bragg Highway 20 line, the river becomes boatable (for white-water experts only) at Branscomb. This run has a rather confined season, however, which falls between the waterway's rambunctious winter floods and its mid-June dry-down.

Halfway between the Pacific Coast and Highway 101, straight west of Laytonville, the narrow river parallels the road to Branscomb for about half of the way. The best access is 3 miles north of the town, where the road to Westport crosses the river. The next 18 miles cascade through protected land owned by the Nature Conservancy, broad and majestic forested slopes untouched by the ravaging lumber interests. This stream area provides the South Fork with its only real head as the river drops quickly from the highlands. These tumultuous beginnings are too much of a challenge to the beginning boater, be he in kayak or canoe, the run of 18 miles to The Hermitage at Rattlesnake Creek is classed as a combination III–IV, suitable only for kayaks, decked white-water canoes, and rafts. At least three or four of the rapids on this run go slightly beyond Class IV. Unless a touring group is liberally sprinkled with experts, these stretches should probably be portaged. Low water, beginning in late May, leaves some of the course nothing more than tough boulder fields and even more dangerous.

The Hermitage to South Fork
(*66 miles* • CLASS I–III • *Running Time 18 hours*)
USGS 15 minute quadrangle maps
"Piercy," "Garberville," and "Weott"

• Access for this run is either at The Hermitage, a mile off
101 and 3 miles south of Leggett, or 5 miles further north, where
the road to the coast and Fort Bragg cuts across the river, half
a mile west of Leggett. Put-ins are numerous above or below
the bridge.

The rating for this stretch can be deceiving, for it is really
a prime beginner's run.

The chief worry for the succeeding 30 miles to Garberville,
or the 25 more to South Fork, is low water anytime after early
June. It is ideal water for casual family groups, with only three
exceptions to the Class II rating. The first of these Class III
drops is about a quarter of a mile downstream from the first
cart-crossing cable. Inexperienced groups should portage around
the boulder-strewn right bank, a short 25-yard carry. The run can
also be negotiated in an open canoe by making a take-out in
a slight eddy on a sand spit just above the first chute on the
far left bank. After a close look, you can drop your boat through
the angled chute, maintaining only enough speed to keep
steerage. A sharp cut to the left between protruding rocks downstream from the drop then carries you into the choppy run below.
A quiet, sylvan glade as you round a sharp S-bend 4 miles from
the launch site is a favorite drinking and browsing spot for deer.

All along the upper half of the 35-mile run to Garberville
the banks are covered with tiny, sparkling waterfalls cascading
over moss-covered rocks. Lush ferns sprout from a hundred un-
seen springs. Though parts of this once-pristine canyon are now
marked with bare slopes from massive bank failures in the 1964
flood and from highway construction, it is still worth seeing.

One of the other two trouble spots is just a few hundred yards
downstream of a large Benbow Inn sign high above the east or
right bank of the river. The sign marks 15 miles to the lake
and its small summer dam. The rapids here are a rocky Class
III, nearly impassable in anything less than high water and one
that should be portaged by open canoes. It is a short and easy
carry on either side. The drop comes at the end of a broad flat
pool, and the worst part is hidden from view until it is too late
to veer off to shore.

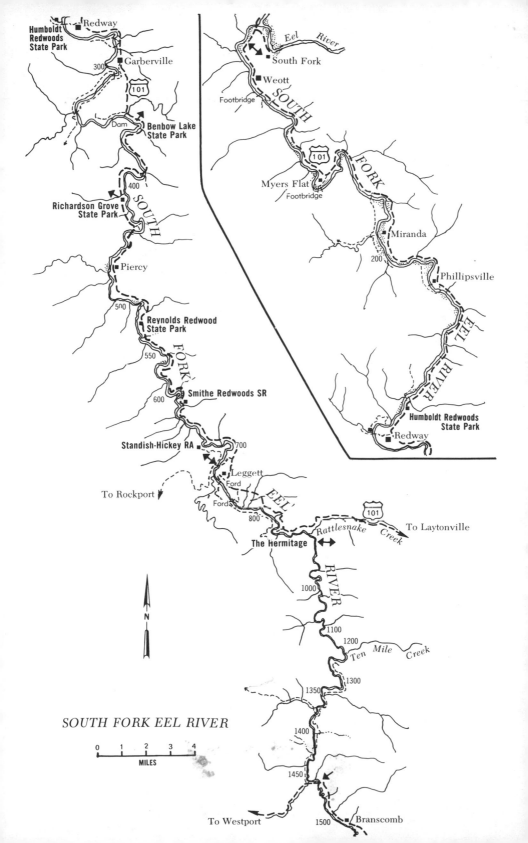

Redway

Humboldt
Redwoods
State Park

300

Garberville

101

Dam

Benbow Lake
State Park

400

SOUTH

Richardson Grove
State Park

Piercy

500

Reynolds Redwood
State Park

550

FORK

600

Smithe Redwoods SR

Standish-Hickey RA

700

Leggett
Ford

To Rockport

Fords

800

EEL

The Hermitage

Eel   River

South Fork

Weott

Footbridge

SOUTH

101

Myers Flat

Footbridge

Miranda

200

Phillipsville

FORK

EEL

RIVER

Humboldt Redwoods
State Park

Redway

101

To Laytonville

Rattlesnake   Creek

RIVER

1000

1100

1200

Ten   Mile   Creek

1300

1350

1400

1450

SOUTH FORK EEL RIVER

0   1   2   3   4
MILES

N

To Westport

1500   Branscomb

We gyrated wildly through the first two narrow drops but hung up on a submerged rock hidden by a crest of foam. The force of the current swung our 15-footer broadside, pinned it against two rocks, and filled it rapidly with water. It took all the strength we could muster to swing the bow up high enough to let the current work against the stern and help pull it free so we could get to shore and bail out.

The next 11 or 12 miles is a peaceful and pretty succession of crystal-clear pools, hooked together by light, bouncy riffles.

The stream abounds with inviting swimming holes, a variety of other bird life, and, in early spring, the swarming lamprey eels. Several times you will have to pile over the side to get clearance through shallow stretches, although staying to the high-bank side on most of them provides deeper water.

The final portage, a must for all but decked craft or rafts, is just below an old gravel quarry on the right side as the canyon begins to flatten out. One more ridgeline and 6 more miles away is Benbow Inn Lake. The upper half of this last rapids can be run most easily on the far left side, angling tightly around the most predominant boulder and then dropping through a tight chute between rocks in midstream. Immediately below the drop, boaters must veer slightly right or left to avoid submerged rocks not readily seen. The rest of the rapids is an impassable boulder patch for about 35 yards. Most feasible portage path is along the right shore, taking out in the pool just above the start of the boulder field.

From here it is just 8 more miles to Garberville, where stately redwood groves flank the scenic stream and state parks offer choice camping facilities and access. A short portage around the right bank of the summer dam at Benbow Lake is the only obstacle of note. The dam is not usually put up until the final week or so of the boating season. The river gradient from Garberville to the junction with the Main branch at South Fork is less than 10 feet per mile. It is a peaceful, easy run in late spring but quickly becomes too shallow for enjoyable boating in early June.

Camping points along this run are too numerous to mention. Picnic tables and fire pits are visible from the river 10 miles below Leggett. Several miles further on, and on the right shore, is the Reynolds Redwood State Park, another magical place of towering trees, verdant ferns, and lush undergrowth. Richardson Grove and Benbow Lake State Parks are other choices.

Sierra Nevada Rivers

The American River
(*100 miles* • CLASS I–V)

SINCE the first nuggets were plucked from its rocky banks in the gold discovery of 1848, the name of the American River has been on the lips of Californians. Now, it's the boating clan that flocks to its banks, seeking pleasure of another kind. Unfortunately for the open canoeist but fortunately for kayakers and rafters, what they find along this bumptious mountain spillway is some of the finest and most demanding white water in the state.

Springing out of the snow-capped Sierra above the storied Mother Lode country, the river tumbles precipitously through deep, narrow canyons and wooded slopes with an average gradient of 120 feet per mile for the first 50 miles. Its three main forks stream into the Sacramento River on the outskirts of the capital city. Forty-eight miles upstream, the Middle and North forks converge, while 30 miles up, the shorter South Fork flows in. While its length along either fork is close to 100 miles, much of the distance is unfit for any boating, either because of the rapid fall of the river or because of the 15 hydroelectric and diversions dams along the way. Many stretches in between these damworks are almost bone dry as the flow is diverted through tubes and tunnels to feed turbines below or over the next ridge.

The river's extended flood runout also inhibits boating from March to June, when most of its annual yield of 2.7 million acre-feet comes spilling down from the mountains. The following runs are those still in use despite the efforts of the dam builders.

South Fork–Kyburz to Folsom Lake
(*35 miles* • CLASS I–V • *Running Time 12 hours*)
USGS 15 minute quadrangle maps
"Robbs Peak" and "Saddle Mtn."

• Nearly all of this tumultuous stretch is strictly out of bounds for open canoes. In fact, there is little water above Chili Bar safe or suitable for anything less than expert kayakers. From the Highway 193 bridge at Chili Bar to Folsom, however, the South Fork has become an important and popular boating section. The first 6 miles to Coloma are Class IV in the highwater of spring, safe only for decked canoes, kayaks, and rafts. Advanced canoeists and small rafts can also handle its boulder fields during low water in late summer.

The only suitable open-canoe running is from Coloma to where the river makes a sharp left turn, heading down into a canyon below and left of Highway 49, about 3.5 miles north of the bridge at Lotus. Total distance of this run from the put-in at Coloma is 6 river miles. The only stiff rapids on this section is about halfway between Coloma and Lotus. It is a short but powerful Class III-IV racemill appropriately called "Old Scary" by the locals. It should be portaged by less than advanced boaters.

The remainder of this open-canoe run is a comparatively easy Class I-II that is nicely suited to a training run. Caution must be taken, however, to flag-mark the take-out point below Highway 49, because the next 10 miles to Folsom Lake are far beyond the scope of open canoes, and even of some kayaks during the heavy spring flow. After the river level subsides in late spring and early summer, however, this gorge run turns into one of the more scenic and exciting kayak and raft runs in the state.

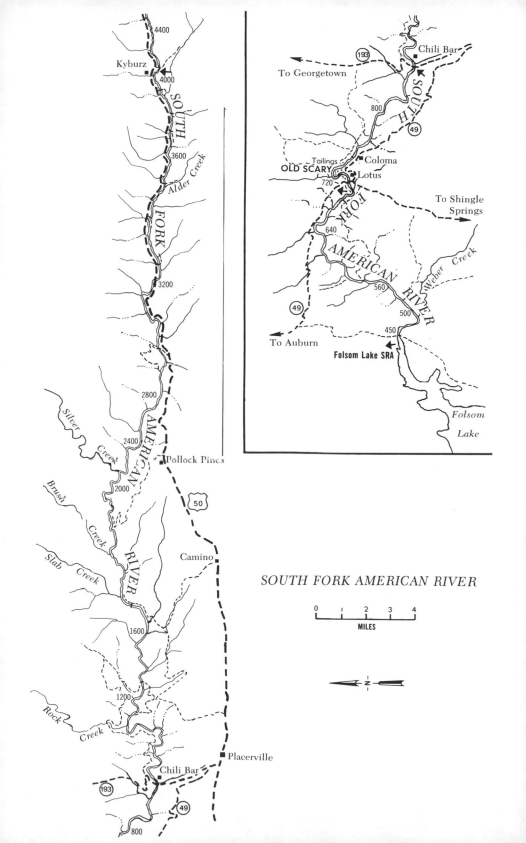

SOUTH FORK AMERICAN RIVER

0 1 2 3 4
MILES

Middle Fork–Forest Hill to Folsom
(26.5 miles • CLASS II–VI • *Running Time 7 hours)*
USGS 15 minute quadrangle maps
"Georgetown" and "Auburn"

• The new Auburn Dam, and the huge reservoir it will back up, will wipe out this entire run, except for the top 14 miles, from Forest Hill to Ruck-a-Chucky Rapids, a Class IV-V stretch. The dam will also wipe out all of the known runs on the North Fork.

Kayakers and rafters may put in for this Middle Fork run from American Bar, which is reached by taking Mosquito Ridge Road out of Forest Hill and then a small side road down to the river. This run is dangerous Class V-VI water during the heavy spring flow, at least 1,600 cubic feet per second.

Not the least of the obstacles along this section is a 300-foot-long tunnel about a mile of swift water below the launch spot. The approach to the entrance is swift, and at high water there could be a deadly lack of clearance. At low water, there is about 8-10 feet of clearance, and the quiet pool at the tunnel's exit is easily visible. Best procedure here is a pull-out before the steep drop to the tunnel mouth and an investigation of the natural but rocky chute to the side, seeking a safe path or the best portage.

There is at least one portage around a boulder field well below the tunnel, and a series of three or four rapids with a IV rating before nearly 2 miles of flat run-out water above Ruck-a-Chucky. When Auburn Dam backs up, this will likely be the upper limit of quiet water. Meanwhile, Ruck-a-Chucky, itself, must be by-passed. It starts out with crushing 10- and 15-foot drops into massive boulders before reaching the Old Greenwood bridge site.

The real loss to open canoes is the lower 18 miles to Folsom, starting from the site of the Old Greenwood bridge, 11.8 miles upstream from the confluence of the North and Middle forks and reached from the Todd Valley-Forest Hill Road by turning off down to the river on McKeon Road.

A late spring run along this 18-mile stretch is rated Class II, with the occasional Class III to Mammoth Bar. The gradient is 15–20 feet to the mile and the river is mostly a succession of beautiful pools and smooth glides, linked by rambunctious chutes and short rapids.

If the dam is not yet finished and you try this run, it is essential

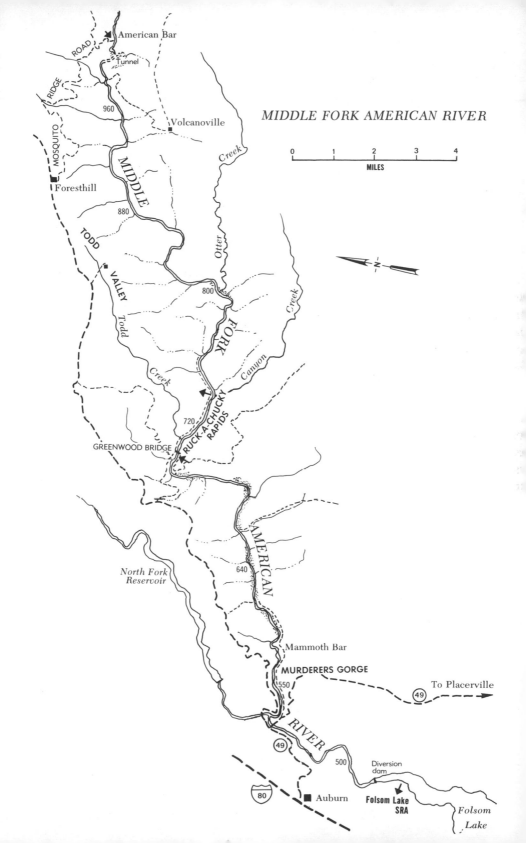

MIDDLE FORK AMERICAN RIVER

American Bar

Tunnel

ROAD

RIDGE

960

Volcanoville

MOSQUITO

MIDDLE

Foresthill

Otter

Creek

880

TODD

800

VALLEY

Todd

FORK

Canyon

Creek

Creek

720

RUCK-A-CHUCKY RAPIDS

GREENWOOD BRIDGE

AMERICAN

North Fork
Reservoir

640

Mammoth Bar

MURDERERS GORGE

550

To Placerville

49

RIVER

49

500

Diversion
dam

80

Auburn

Folsom Lake
SRA

Folsom
Lake

0   1   2   3   4
MILES

N

that you take the time to drive down to the river at Mammoth Bar first—a dirt road turnoff about 5 miles from the river junction—and place a marking flag or wide strip of colorful cloth to mark the take-out. For just below this run is Murderer's Gorge, well-named for its deadly lacework of boulders and treacherous currents. This is not runable at any water level. The portage, on an old private road on the right side of the river, is long but not too taxing. And it opens up a 4-mile, easy run-out to the confluence.

There is one steep chute just opposite the big quarry works that might have to be walked around, and the sweeping S-turn, just as the high, arching Highway 49 bridge comes into view, should also be portaged, on the right side. Following this portage, there is an 8-mile Class II run-out to Folsom. A rough comber section appears on the right, just below the confluence, and boaters should stay to the left. The same applies to another pitch 400 yards downstream, where a walk-by may be needed. About 3 miles downstream is the only other hazard, an old diversion dam breached on both banks with a swift and dangerous approach. Portage on the right and then there is mostly quiet water onward to Folsom Lake.

MAIN BRANCH
(*24 miles* • CLASS I–II)

Nimbus Dam to Discovery Park
(*24 miles* • CLASS I–II • *Running Time 7 hours*)
USGS 15 minute quadrangle maps
"Folsom" and "Fair Oaks"

• This river run is a perfect graduation from the Russian River for the beginner and is used as such by many canoe clubs. It is bigger, swifter and offers a variety of fast water, although there is almost always plenty of room to maneuver in or to draw clear of the faster rapids. The popularity of this run has attracted a canoe rental agency, American River Canoe Trips, on the north side of the river, a quarter of a mile downstream of the first bridge below the dam. The rental area has a good launching spot—a small natural lagoon or backwater just off the main current. Along the run, there are a host of take-out points at any of the eight highway bridges you pass beneath, including the Fair Oaks Boulevard, Sunrise Boulevard, Watt Avenue, H Street,

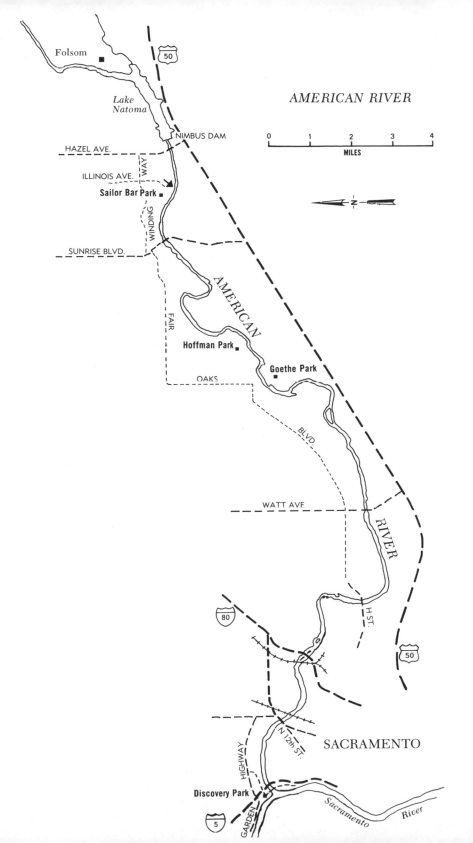

U. S. 99, North 12th Street, and finally, the Jibboon Street or Garden Highway at the river's confluence with the mighty Sacramento. However, the 24-mile trip is best suited to an overnight run, with a camping stop at Gothe Park, 12 miles downriver from the put-in and on the left bank about 150-200 yards from the water. You'll find water and fireplaces there.

The access point to begin this adventure is the same as that of the rental agency, reached by taking Highway 50 east out of Sacramento to the Hazel Avenue off-ramp east of the city, turning left to cross the American on the Hazel Street bridge. Across the bridge, turn left on Winding Way, then left again about a quarter of a mile further on at Illinois Avenue. Take this route down to Sailor Bar County Park, where there is easy access to the water.

Halfway down the first 12-mile leg of the tour, the river splits around a huge island. Beginners should take the left-hand fork, where there is nothing more than a mild rapids. More expert boaters can enjoy a more challenging run on the right, being careful not to get trapped in a jam of wood and debris which the current leaves on the right bank in the middle of a sweeping left turn.

Thereafter, it is another 3 miles to the only challenging water along this section of river—a rock-ledge drop, nearly river wide, which is at the bottom of a gradual right turn and a rocky outcropping with a large, flat, gravel bar poking out on the left. The entire ledge is impassable in all but early-spring water. Then there are chutes at either end, the one on the left much the better of the two.

Approaching this "gate," boaters must start out just barely right of the center slick, slicing off to the left from the foot of a beginning boil against an upthrust rock. This angling maneuver should be strong and long enough to carry you past the rolling combers at the base of the chute but not so far as to get you caught in the very strong reverse coming back along the near shore to the left. You should ride out the 200 yards of swift chop below, almost all the way to its end. Too quick a pull-out for a shortcut across the sweeping bend will thrust you into the opposing current of the back eddy.

From there to the take-out at Discovery Park, it is merely a matter of dodging shad anglers in the spring, salmon and steelhead fishermen in the fall months, and swimmers in the summer.

Novices take a mild wipe-out on this mild chute of
the American River between Nimbus Dam and
Fair Oaks, above Sacramento. A long, placid pool
below offered a safe run-out for the dislodged
boaters. This modest upset experience gives
beginners confidence in how to handle themselves
in moments of possible duress.

The Consumnes River
(75 miles • CLASS I–V)

THIS sparkling river flows most of its length through a rocky canyon and a succession of gorges that make its water among the cleanest of any river in the West. And the fact that it is still without any major damworks adds to its wild-river flavor. Although it was a prolific producer of placer gold in its 49er days, the Consumnes has a comparatively small watershed—less than 600 square miles—and, therefore, a rather limited prime boating season. Still, most boaters can handle the river through the whole month of July.

Its upper boating limit is at Highway E16, between Somerset and Melson's Corner, northeast of Plymouth and Highway 49. This is, be assured, strictly tiger country. Rafts with rowing frames could cope with its wild chutes and funnels through rocky gorges, and kayaks and decked European C-1s might be able to handle the conditions in May and June. But anyone who ventures this high up in an open canoe is headed for trouble.

Highway E16 to Highway 49
(15 miles • CLASS IV–V • Running Time 7 hours)
USGS 15 minute quadrangle maps
"Camino" and "Placerville"

• For rafts, decked canoes, and kayaks, there is good launch room from the foot of the old bridge on Highway E16, at the south bank. There is a rough drop half a mile below and several hundred yards more of fairly rough going, but this is merely heavy water with no obstructions. The river flattens out and snakes along the valley floor for another mile, between steepening walls. Then you pick up the unmistakable low-pitched sound of falling water.

Small diversion dam near summer resort
community of Outlanding is the first of several
impassable sections of the upper Consumnes River
as it tumbles down the steepening west slope of
the Sierras below Placerville. Suitable for kayaks
and small rafts in late spring and early
summer—in wet years—this part of the river is
out of bounds for open canoes.

A diversion dam, to feed pumps serving the resort community of Outingdale, another mile below, backs the water up into a small, gem-like lake. Looking ahead, you can see the pronounced downward break in the landscape. The portage pullout should be made on the left, 20 yards upstream of the brink, for an easy 100-yard carry. A mile below the 15-foot high dam, the river drifts by some handsome summer cabins, one of which has an underwater wood-and-rock dam to form a swimming pool. This would have to be passed on the far right at low water, just clearing the rocks poking up from below, 3 yards from shore.

There is a very tight S-turn 30 yards below to the left that in 1970 was guarded in midstream by a big snag. Passage is best just to the right of center, watching out for big underwater rocks two thirds of the way through on the right.

Care must be taken to skirt the right edge of the current on the tail of this S-turn, since the current cuts straight into a bank and then blunders off to the right, forming a strong reverse. Just beyond is another sharp left turn and drop, with very tight passage down a small slick between upthrust rocks just off the left shore.

From there on, the river tumbles through a gorge. The gradient for the next 6 miles is between 80 and 120 feet per mile, with some powerful and sudden drops. When the water drops in July, it becomes an impassable boulder field most of the way.

Highway 49 to Highway 49 Bridge
(*9 miles* • CLASS II • *Running Time 3 hours*)
USGS 15 minute quadrangle map *"Placerville"*

• Open canoes can pick up this very beautiful North Fork by turning to the right off Highway 49 (northbound) just 1½ miles north of the small roadside town of Nashville and where 49 jogs to the left. The small road leading straight ahead should be followed for another 1½ miles to a point where the river is only 80 feet away and you can see it coming down from the 800-foot deep gorge to the east. There is closer access than this (via the first right-hand turnoff a mile north of Nashville to a bridge), but it shortens the run by about 2½ miles.

The gradient for this run through beautiful, soft, rolling hills eases back to an enjoyable 10–15 feet per mile. Trout fishing

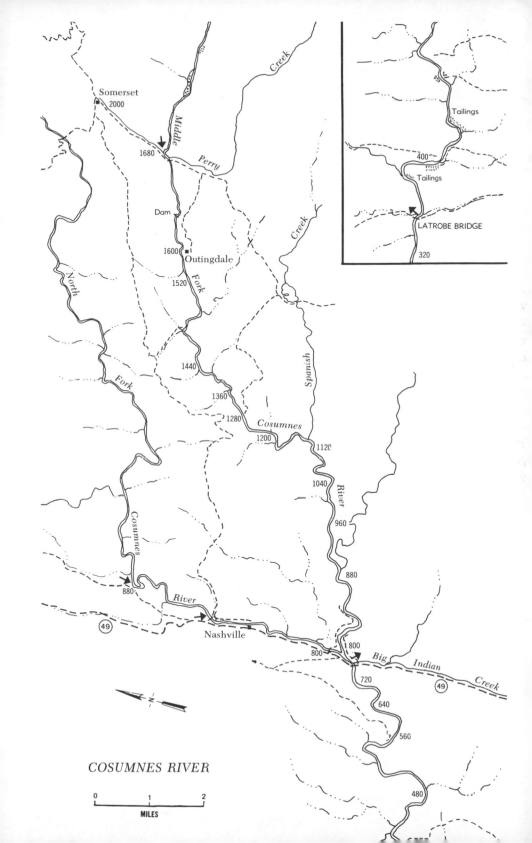

COSUMNES RIVER

MILES

0   1   2

is great in late spring and early summer with both bait and flies in this area. The rapids are mostly short, bouncy chutes free of obstruction. The riverbed is predominantly gravel.

The take-out must come at the confluence with the river's smaller Middle Fork, just upstream of the Highway 49 bridge and on the left bank. those who want one more nice rapid can shoot the one right underneath the bridge but must then make their take-out in the pool on the right bank. The hike back up to the road is not too steep.

Below here, the river slams its way down over the lip of the Sierra's lower foothills and piles into a rugged gorge, plummeting 160 feet in the first 1½ miles. It might be an exciting run for rafts with rowing frames and expert handlers. Canoes must definitely avoid this part of the river, and it should be scouted extensively by any others before running. April is too early for anything but rafts here.

Even after this first gorge, the descent is 80 feet for the next mile and then gradually tapering off to 20 or 30 feet all the way to the Latrobe Road bridge.

Latrobe Bridge to Bridgehouse
(*9 miles* • CLASS III–IV • *Running Time 4½ hours*)
USGS 15 minute quadrangle maps
"Placerville," "Folsom," and "Carbondale"

• This is not beginner's country either. In fact, during the heavy spring flow, this part of the Consumnes should probably be considered a steady Class IV. By June, it can be considered a basic Class III, but there are still some very tough spots. The upper 4 miles slide down the rim of the east side of the valley at 25-30 feet per mile.

Just 400 yards below the Latrobe bridge and its peaceful pool, the river bends to the left into a smooth glide and then tumbles head over heels through an impassable cascade. Portage is mandatory on the right bank for at least half a mile in order to bypass a later set of drops that could be handled at low water only by decked craft manned with advanced intermediates. After the last of this series of cascades, all within a few hundred yards of each other, the river settles down to a good Class II for the 4 to 5 miles to Michigan Bar bridge. The gradient is only 10 feet to the mile.

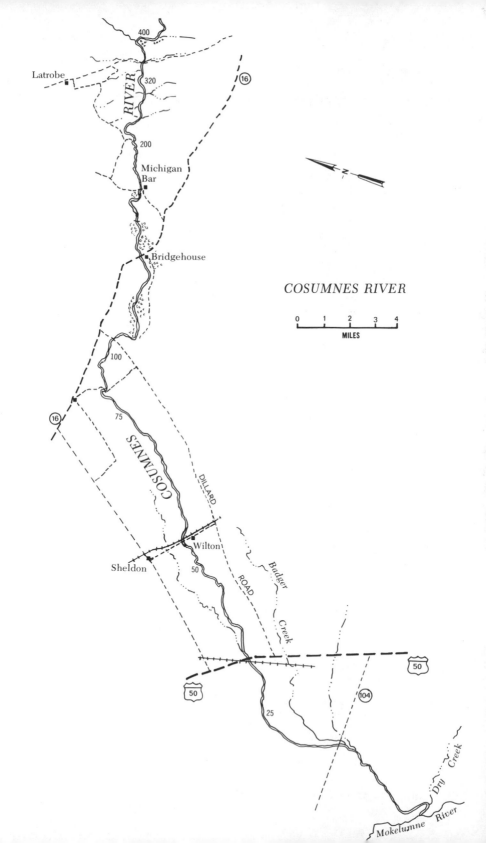

COSUMNES RIVER

Two miles beyond the Michigan Bar bridge, there is a diversion dam with spillways on either side of an island around which the river forks. It is a drop of 15 feet, but the approach to the brink is slow and easy, best on the right side where the quiet water is more pronounced. From there to Bridgehouse, where Highway 16 to Sloughhouse crosses, is a peaceful run-out at a descent of only 5 feet per mile.

Bridgehouse to U.S. 99
(22 miles • CLASS I • Running Time 7 hours)
USGS 15 minute quadrangle maps
"Sloughhouse" and "Franklin"

• In early spring, with flood run-out, this portion of the river can be two classes higher. In April, for example, it carries a current of 4 to 5 miles per hour and features one very exciting rapids that almost ranks as Class III because of the height of its waves and the depth of its combers over at least 200 yards.

The put-in, at Bridgehouse, can be from either side. With permission of the Bridgehouse Store owners, cars can be parked in a large yard and canoes walked down to the south bank just downstream of the highway bridge. To gain access to the north bank, permission must be obtained to drive through gates leading to a huge heavy equipment school for apprentices, which is 200 yards north of the bridge. Cars can be driven from there right down to the rock levy.

There are some spicy little riffles on this run during the first few miles. Even late in the year, when the water is considerably thinned down, the depth and current are probably enough to provide a comfortable float. In 1970, we were forced to dart for shore rounding a left turn where the current spits out a big peaceful backwater. A huge oak tree had blown down, stretching all the way across the channel. The same thing happened on another narrow turn just downstream of the Dillard Road bridge linking Wilton to Highway 16 at Sloughhouse.

There is a second take-out for the shorter, 9-mile Shoughhouse run at another bridge, 2 miles downstream of the Dillard Road crossing. We made this full run in one day, thanks to the strong spring current. The next 13 miles to U. S. 99 is slower water and, like that above, flanked by an almost solid wall of willows and oak trees harboring a variety of bird life.

One of the state's last "uncontrolled" rivers, the
Consumnes becomes a perfect piece of open canoe
water as it flows peacefully through the broad
farming plains of the Central Valley, from
Bridgehouse to its confluence with the Mokelumne
River. As its blue-crystal depths show here, it is
one of the valley's cleanest and most scenic
streams. Boating season lasts through early
summer.

The one piece of big water comes just below an abandoned bridge 3 miles downstream from Sloughhouse. In spring, it is a surprising river-wide surge of whitecaps and rollers breaking over a series of rock ledges. Before proceeding through, beginners should make a take-out above the bridge on the right for a careful look.

While it will look ominous to beginners, the stretch should be quite easily handled. Simply ease over to the left bank beneath the bridge and follow the angling ledge about 4 yards offshore. Then take to the slick for the first pronounced chute and break through the following combers for a straight and exciting run. There are at least three other shorter rapids between here and the highway, but they are no challenge, even to beginners.

There are several good take-out points on this lower part of the river. For a shorter and more ideal one-day trip, boaters should pull to shore at the second bridge after negotiating the abandoned-bridge run. The first is a trestle for the Central California Traction Railroad and provides no vehicular access. The Sheldon-Wilton road crossing is about 3 miles beyond. Canoes should be beached on the right bank and upstream side of the bridge for an easy walk up to a dirt frontage road leading to county road E2 and Sheldon. From there you have access to Highway 99 and are less than 20 miles south of Sacramento.

The E2 road take-out can also serve as a put-in point for a full day of placid paddling along the meandering Consumnes for 14 miles to Thornton. This trip takes you under the U.S. 99 bridge—an optional take-out or launching site—and, several miles beyond, to two more crossings, Highway 104 and the Lower Stockton road, near Thornton. However, anything beyond that point, and later than the heavier spring flow, is slower yet and subject to tidal action. Yet, the stretch can be most rewarding to bird lovers because of the huge egret and heron rookeries near the confluence with the Mokelumne River and the Delta tidewater.

The Merced River
(*84 miles* • CLASS II–V)

WHAT John Muir had to say in trying to adequately describe the incomparable beauty of the Upper Merced hasn't been improved upon over the years:

> The [Yosemite] park includes the headwaters of the Tuolumne and the Merced rivers, two of the most songful streams in the world; innumerable lakes and waterfalls and smooth silky lawns; the noblest forests, the loftiest granite domes, the deepest ice-sculptured canyons, the brightest crystalline pavements and snow mountains soaring into the sky twelve and thirteen thousand feet, arrayed in open ranks and spiry pinnacled groups partially separated by tremendous canyons and amphitheaters; gardens on their sunny brows, avalanches thundering down their long white slopes, cataracts roaring gray and foaming in the crooked, rugged gorges.

Muir's sentence is as breathtaking as the scenery it describes.

One of the last sections of untamed water in the state, the Upper Merced, as it meanders back and forth through the scenic Yosemite Valley, is highly prized by all boaters. Unfortunately, portions of the river are neither available nor safe for all boaters. The upper 8-mile stretch in the park itself is closed to all boating. The National Park Service is naturally leery about the use of the river by careless novices and, thus far, has kept the prohibition a firm policy. However, other national parks in the country are beginning to see the high recreational value of such uses of the waterways, and the Yosemite superintendent has been approached about implementing some kind of permit system for boating on the river. Canoeing organizations may well have to launch a planned joint program to win the opening of this most scenic of all river waters in California.

Much of the Merced is a beautiful Class II with occasional Class III drops. Only for a short stretch near Happy Isle does the Merced range beyond advanced beginner status. There, through a series of chutes and drops, it reaches a Class III–V rating. Below the park boundary, the Merced is available and presents a variety of classifications as it tumbles quickly down the western slope of the Sierra toward the valley.

El Portal to Indian Flat Campground
(6 miles • CLASS III–IV • *Running Time 1½ hours)*
USGS 15-minute quadrangle map *"El Portal"*

• This section, paralleling Highway 140, is a demanding series of drops and rapids that exceed the capability of an open canoe, no matter how practiced the paddlers are. Rated Class III–IV at even moderately low water, it should be strictly off-limits for all but the most advanced boater during high spring water. The descent on this stretch exceeds 100 feet per mile in several spots, and there is seldom any pause in the steady downhill run.

The snow-fed river, still wild and untamed here, runs bank-full only during the heavy snow melt in late May and June. Both before and after, depending upon the weather and the winter snowpack, the river has a comfortable head of water. In the very late summer, there is a good possibility that the stream will become too thin.

Indian Flat to Briceburg
(12.2 miles • CLASS II–III • *Running Time 3 hours)*
USGS 15-minute quadrangle map *"El Portal"*

• The Merced pauses here in a scenic canyon to catch its breath. Although there are four solid Class III rapids on this run—including one that approaches a IV and two that may have to be portaged by open canoes during lower water after July—between these cascades there are long stretches of quiet pools, interspersed with a succession of challenging but fun Class II runs.

The lower and more peaceful stretches of the
Merced River, from Merced Falls to McConnell
State Park, are flanked by towering oak trees and
provide one of the more popular "lazy runs" in
the Central Valley rivers.

Marking Indian Flat as mile 0, there is a Class III rapid just .2 mile downstream. It is about 200 yards long and forked, joining again between two large submerged boulders. The left fork is best and should be run along its left-of-center course. Then be sure to split the center slick when the forks join again.

At mile .6 is another Class III rapid, this time 300 yards long and demanding passage on the far-left side between submerged and surface rocks. It is tricky but not dangerous. Less than half a mile below, a short drop in the middle of an S-curve takes the current up against protruding shore rocks on the right and forces the boater to quarter left across the current to clear the turbulence.

At mile 1.1, a shallow run presents some maneuverability challenges, although it would be less of an obstacle in the higher water before mid-July. The best route is to hug the right hand bank until the river swings left around an imposing rock pile, then veer over the bumps just to right of midstream and pull right next to the left bank at the base of the shallow stretch. To finish this maneuver, one must break out to the center of the stream, 200 yards below the base of the shallow stretch, and then catch a left-to-right sideslip between large boulders providing no more than 6 feet of clearance.

At the base of an S-curve, half a mile down, stay to the far left on the upper half, veering right two thirds of the way down to miss large surface rocks. The small drop 75 yards below should be taken right through the middle into the long quiet pool below. There, hugging close to the midstream willows that mark the upper end of the curving drop, boaters should quarter quickly left across the current as they enter the white water, in order to catch a pile-up slick that bypasses the rather sharp drop on the right. These directions are mainly for the less maneuverable open canoes, of course. Kayaks face few, if any, real obstacles through these runs.

Just below where the South Fork of the Merced comes in from the left, there is a long shallow stretch for which the deepest passage is along the right bank of a narrow island. The lower end of the run may have to be waded. During low water, a similar wade or portage might also be needed further down, where the river courses to the right through a boulder field for several hundred yards.

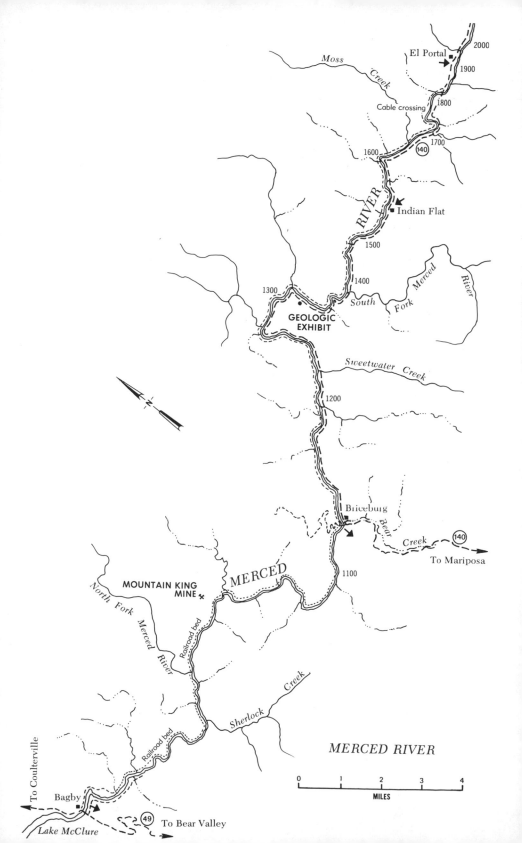

MERCED RIVER

Two hundred yards further downstream, another fork offers a right side that is very narrow and marked with strong waves. The quieter left fork, however, needs a portage at its base around a sharp, impassable ledge. Beyond this point, at mile 4.2, there is an almost river-wide drop over another ledge that would be comparatively easy at higher water; but with low water, passage is safe only right in the center. The exposed rust-colored rock cliff on the left, above Highway 140, is the oldest geologic formation in the park. In fact, this is the worn-down nub of the original prehistoric Sierra.

Canoes must portage at the run's only Class IV drop, which is marked by a white cabin on the right bank, and the first cabin to come into view on this stretch. The river turns sharply to the left through a steep-walled canyon. Make your take-out on the right hand bar above the white water and portage a quarter of a mile to a quiet, deep pool below. This area provides some prized trout angling for those who want to break out the rods and reels. Bait in the day or flies early mornings or late evenings are the best producers for trout to 14 inches.

From the portage, the gradient slows noticeably, and the next mile is one of the easiest parts of the river. At Mile 11.6, the Merced turns right into narrow forks, with the best route on the right side all the way. No further obstacles arise before the take-out at Briceburg, which can be identified by an abandoned white-stone gas station and store on the left, just downstream of Bear Creek bridge. Other noticeable markers are a suspension bridge straight ahead and the cabin it leads to on the north bank. If you are a believer in signs, the owner of the cabin is not fond of interruptions or trespassers, so take-out should be limited to the left bank on the upstream side of Bear Creek. The highway is only a few yards away from here.

Briceburg to Highway 49
(14 miles • CLASS IV–V • *Running Time 5 hours)*
USGS 15 minute quadrangle map *"Coulterville"*

• From Briceburg, the Merced slants away from the highway and piles head over keel down a long, isolated rocky canyon. It is absolutely a no-man's land for open canoes and suitable

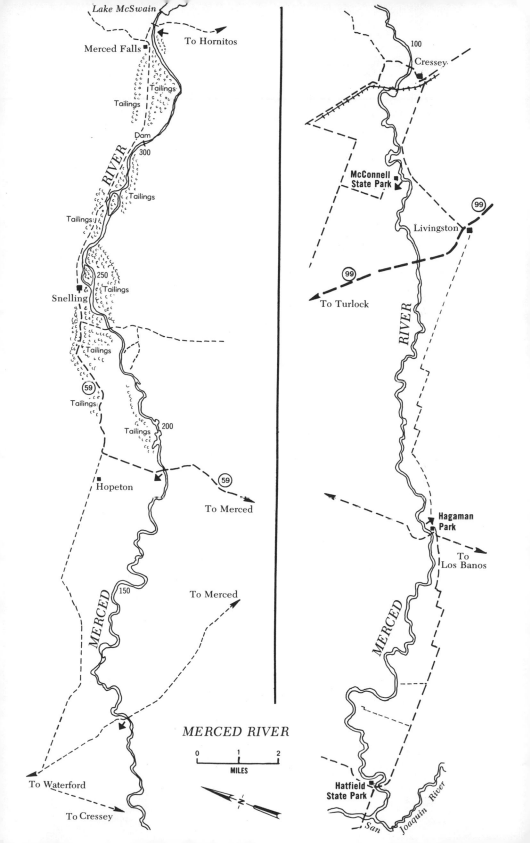

Lake McSwain

To Hornitos

Merced Falls

Tailings

Tailings

RIVER

Tailings

Dam

300

Tailings

Tailings

250

Tailings

Snelling

Tailings

Tailings

59

Tailings

Tailings

200

Hopeton

59

To Merced

150

MERCED

To Merced

To Waterford

To Cressey

MERCED RIVER

0   1   2

MILES

N

100

Cressey

McConnell
State Park

99

Livingston

99

To Turlock

RIVER

Hagaman
Park

To
Los Banos

MERCED

Hatfield
State Park

San   Joaquin   River

only for top hands in decked craft or rafts. During the heavier spring run-off, this run reaches Class V–VI difficulty, with at least one impassable obstacle—a 20-foot-high waterfall about 9 miles into the canyon. Even at the lower water levels of late spring and early summer, which is the best running time for advanced paddlers, the rating of this stretch of the Merced stays at Class IV–V.

The put-in for this run would be the east or upstream side of Bear Creek, just before Highway 140 loops up and away from the river. The only semblance of a road from there on is the old railroad bed that parallels the river. This grade offers comfortable footing for portages and also provides a fine scouting perch for the many miles of tough white water and obstacles, such as the diversion dam of the abandoned King gold mine. Breached in several places, the dam still has a navigable chute in the center, although the conditions vary with the water flow and should be scouted.

Below the dam, the longest and most difficult series of drops and chutes begin—most of them Class V at high water and probably requiring portage. A waterfall is just beyond the last of these rapids and is definitely not passable. Portage is on the right.

As a result of the Lake McClure Dam, the last 3½ miles of this run are flat paddling through rather arid, barren gorges. Still, there is isolation here and rugged beauty of a sort; and in the cool of the morning or early evening, the lunkers come upstream from the lake for feeding and cooler water, making fishing highly rated here.

There is an ideal take-out at a marina and bait shop on the left bank, just a few hundred yards upstream of the new Highway 49 bridge over the lake.

Merced Falls to McConnell State Park
(30 miles • CLASS I–II • *Running Time 8 hours)*
USGS 15 minute quadrangle maps
"Merced Falls," "Merced," and "Atwater"

• The midsection of the Merced is more to the tastes of the river canoeist. The water is not quite so placid as below, from McConnell to Hagaman State Park, and the active current makes the work against upriver afternoon winds less burdensome. There is a good access to an ideal put-in spot just below the PG&E powerhouse, on Highway J17 east of Turlock. A hundred yards below the powerhouse structure, right beside the chain-link fence and on the south side of J17, there is a dirt road leading toward the river. Downstream 150 yards is a parking site adjacent to a crossover cable cart. Canoes can easily be launched down a path to the river 10 yards away.

The first 2 miles of river from that point offer a quiet placid surface, isolated and scenic in the absence of upriver winds, which usually spring up about 2 P.M. On a windy day, however, the paddling can be back-breaking work. The first challenge of any kind on this run comes as you near a dominant cut-bank cliff, towering above the south shore of the river. Unless the water is quite low, all but the most experienced white-water runners should give this an advance casing, pulling to the right shore 100 yards above the drop.

The current funnels into a swift, narrow chute, piling over three tricky and diagonal combers that could swamp the inexperienced or unwary. Comparatively safe passage is possible by cutting across the head of the chute to the right, being careful to avoid getting swept broadside into a large rock at the bottom and about 3 yards from shore. The best maneuver is for the bowman to use a sweeping draw stroke on the left to clear the boulder as the stern man either back-sculls lightly on the right or executes a modified draw, inward and slightly forward. Once the bow is clear of the obstacle on the left, a quick reversal of that sequence must be made in order to bring the stern equally clear—the bow switching from the sweep to a sharp inward draw on the left as the stern makes an out-draw or pushover on the left side.

Caution must be exercised not to overcorrect and get the stern quartered to the current, for the reverse eddy below will tend to swing the boat sharply around and could capsize it. Good insurance in this and similar situations is to make sure you head into the chute at the slowest possible speed, certainly no faster than the current and, sometimes, when the turning room is short, back-paddling to slow down even more. The latter must not be overdone, of course, since the result would be a loss of control and direction.

The river swings sharply right at the base of the chute and

should be run almost dead center or slightly to the right. The succeeding 6 miles are mostly long stretches of nearly still water, interspersed only with mild riffles, but then an irrigation diversion dam blocks the river. It is visible for a long distance upriver. Boats should bear to the left of an island, aiming for a cement blockhouse on the left shore. The water is very slow and there is no danger of being swept over the structure. Portage is easy along a narrow-gauge track from the dam to the shore, and launching spots are numerous below the dam and just above a return bypass drainage canal. Some of the riffles here, and below, are too shallow for running—depending on the amount of flow—and must be waded.

The next 4 miles are a return to slow, placid water, separated by narrow and shallow riffles. The first take-out access point is beneath the Highway 59 bridge; but stopping here would make a rather short run for one day, and the next 5 miles feature a noticeable improvement in the gradient, with more and faster riffles and less paddle work. While some of the runs put a premium on maneuverability in tight quarters around rocks and overhanging brush, there is no danger other than getting tangled up or maybe shipping a little water. The paddle work here is more fun than anything else.

There is one very real hazard on this stretch, however—barbed-wire fences. Unbelievable as it may sound, one rancher has actually fenced the entire breadth of the river with taut, four-strand, barbed-wire barriers. We cleared the first fence by less than an inch, huddled beneath the gunwales. The second, about a mile further on, is impassable. The boater is forced to get out on the right bank and float his boat under, then hold up the lower strand for his own clearance.

Beyond the second fence, the river continues to offer a nice variety of riffles and runs until it flattens out just above the second highway bridge (the Highway 59 cut-off from Amsterdam to Hickman). There is a take-out a quarter of a mile below the bridge on the south bank. Gear must be walked back up a dirt river road to the highway.

From the Highway 59 cut-off bridge, it is another 7 or 8 miles to McConnell State Park, which provides an ideal access point. An earlier stopping-off spot for an overnight run is about 13 miles into the run. While anything above the stream-bed, high-water line at that point is private, there has been no adverse reaction to quiet campers who are cautious about fire hazard and who police up their campsite.

The only real hazard along this section of the Merced would be low water. The flow was close to 800 second-feet when we ran it in late March of 1971. A phone call to either PG&E's watermaster or to the Merced Irrigation District, which operates Exchequer Dam and the lower McSwain Reservoir and power-plant dam, could easily pin down the flow rate. It would be close to impassable at anything much below 500 second-feet.

There is an abundance of bird life along the lower runs. Almost every backwater hides a pair of nesting mallards, and crows, blackbirds, hawks, turkey vultures, owls, and great blue herons are other river inhabitants.

McConnell State Park to Hagaman State Park
(14 miles • CLASS I • Running Time 4½ hours)
USGS 15-minute quadrangle map *"Turlock"*

• The lower Merced, as more and more communities and farming operations add their garbage and waste to the stream, is not fit for man or beast. Nowhere in California are the ravages of man against rivers more painfully apparent. Upriver dams have cut the Merced's lifestream; farmland sediment, pesticide residue, and nutrients have clogged its bottom with layers of poisonous silt; incoming sewers have fouled its purity; and wastes from massive new wineries have dyed its color a sickening muddy purple strong enough to dye your shoes or clothes if you were unfortunate enough to fall in.

Nowhere is there a riffle or spit of white water. The current is almost completely stifled and the banks are an endless refuse heap. Unfortunately, the same can be said for most of the Sierra rivers once they hit the San Joaquin Valley flatlands. The closer they get to the dozens of farming communities and valley cities, the more objectionable they become. As a general rule, the good river running ends about 10 miles east of U. S. 99. Complaints to the State Water Resources Control Board have brought pledges to clamp down harder on dischargers to clean up the valley segments of these fine riverways. Clearly, more complaining is called for.

The Mokelumne River

(*27 miles* • CLASS I-III)

SCOURED from the granite ledges of the Sierra by massive glaciers, the Mokelumne's three main branches slice through deep canyons, leaving a beautiful lacework of sapphire lakes and emerald meadows in its path. Its tumbling headwaters are almost equidistant from Lake Tahoe and Yosemite and of its three forks, the South Fork is the most beautiful, gouging through canyons almost a mile deep in places. Along the banks of these forks lay relics of the fantastic Mother Lode era, including the Amador gold mines that yielded $300 million in gold. Here, the names of Bret Harte, Mark Twain, and the fanciful bandits Joaquin Murieta and Black Bart are intertwined with the history of such places as Jackson, Fiddletown, Volcano, Sutter Creek, Drytown, and Poverty Bar.

Alas, little of the 130-mile length of the Mokelumne is left for boating, so massive is the network of five hydroelectric dams and two huge storage reservoirs, the Pardee and Camanche. There is some small consolation in that the river's few remaining navigable stretches offer prolonged boating because of the controlled flows. It is on the lower sections of the Mokelumne, below Camanche Dam, that these controlled flows at least return some of the dividends stripped from the headwaters. They provide a prolonged and ideal open-canoe boating season, especially suited to beginners.

Camp Electra to Pardee

(*10 miles* • CLASS I-III • *Running Time 2½ hours*)
USGS 15 minute quadrangle maps
"Mokelumne Hill" and "Sutter Creek"

• The most unique aspect on this short but thrilling run from below the PG&E dam at Camp Electra to the headwaters of Pardee Reservoir is that it can be run twice in the same day with entirely different water conditions. It is really two different rivers in one. PG&E backs up water at Electra all night and

Pleasant warmth of the fragrant Central Valley
spring lured these paddlers to a brief pause along
the serene lower Mokelumne River where huge
colonies of herons and egrets nest in the tall oak
trees that drink from the stream's edge.

morning and then begins shunting it out through the generating turbines as the demand for electricity builds toward its 6 P.M. peak-consumption hour. This release schedule causes two-foot-plus fluctuations in the river level every day, and that represents a difference of almost a full class rating.

At its lowest ebb, between 9-10 A.M., the river is passable but tricky for open canoes—the challenges coming mainly from dodging submerged rocks. During this shallow morning run, there are also two chutes that rank as short Class III hurdles. The first is about a third of the way down, where the 30-foot-wide channel funnels into a 12-foot-wide racemill that drops sharply into a frothing chute. There is no difficulty with rocks here, but the waves are both high and powerful.

For open canoes, the only path by which to avoid a good dunking is to the right of the highest combers, but that takes strong mid-course maneuvers to pull out of the brutal main current. We made it halfway through, then hit a big wave and shipped water. The water sloshed far to one side as the next high comber tipped us at a sharp angle and then tilted us almost on edge. Then, the next thing we knew, another white horse kicked our unbalanced bow and we were over.

Another 1½ miles downstream is the run's other Class III chute. The chute is guarded on the right by a jagged underwater rock that could slice a boat badly at lower water and on the left, 5 yards further, by a large submerged boulder that triggers a sharp drop and dangerous reversal. The best course here is to scout the run first, preferably from along the left shore. Then, follow a middle course, pointing at the white frill kicked up by the rock on the right of center but only just enough to clear it. Several quick, powerful strokes on the left by the bowman and some in-draw strokes on the right by the stern paddler will be needed to pull out of the center current and skim past the right side of the large rock.

This is a particularly tough maneuver for rafters, unless the raft is fitted with rowing frames, because of the quickness of the current and the lack of maneuvering time between obstacles. Many rafts seem to be drawn over the sharp lower shelf sideways. There is also some danger of a flip-over here, for the full force of the current piles right down on top of the hole, pinning down anyone floundering right beneath the drop. Remember that later

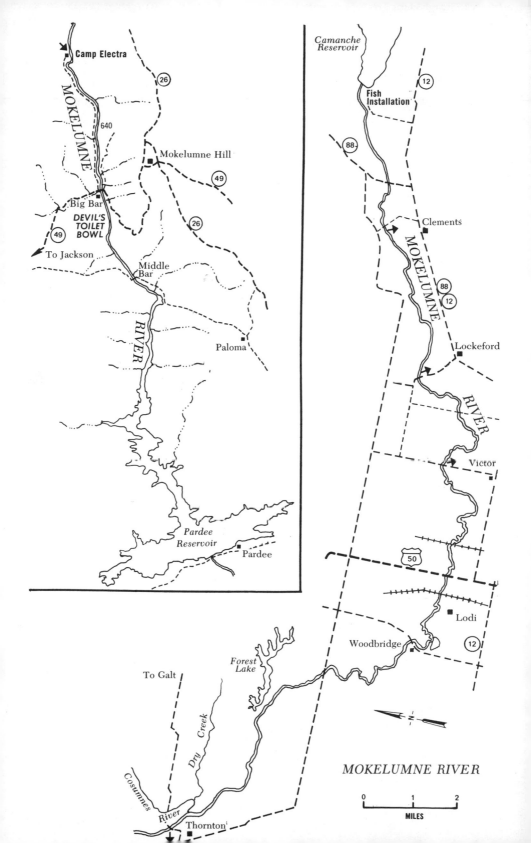

MOKELUMNE RIVER

0 1 2

MILES

in the day, or much earlier in the morning, these chutes should be upgraded to where they must be scouted ahead of time, and possibly even portaged by open canoes.

There is take-out access at the Highway 49 bridge, on the left and upstream side, in case you should like to shuttle the boats back to the initial launching place for another shot at this pleasant run of clear, cold water. You can also continue on downriver toward Pardee or Middle Bar, bouncing over a long and rather tough Class III run just downstream a quarter of a mile from the bridge. The run just down from the bridge is a favorite with rafters and is laughingly called the Devil's Toilet Bowl because of the unusual flushing swirl of some of the drops.

From there to the flat water of the upper end of Pardee, the Mokelumne snakes through an isolated and beautiful wildlife-refuge area that permits fine nature study. This is also highly prized fishing water because of light fishing pressure caused by lack of access between the highway and the reservoir.

Camanche to Victor
(17 miles • CLASS I • Running Time 6 hours)
USGS 15 minute quadrangle maps
"Valley Springs" and "Bellota"

• The put-in here is from just below the Mokelumne River Fish Installation, an artificial salmon and steelhead hatchery built to try to replace the valuable spawning beds covered by the flooding of Camanche Reservoir. Access is by Highway 88 out of Stockton to its junction with Highway 12, just 2 miles east of Clements. Take 12 straight ahead for another mile to the hatchery road, turning north for another 1½ miles, and then take the right fork there to the gravel parking lot on the left. A footpath leads down to a quiet, mirrored pool for perfect launching just above the run's first riffle. The Mokelumne is the clearest of all valley streams, at least on its lower stretches.

There is no fishing allowed this close to the entrance of the spawning channels; but anglers should take along their fly or spin gear in season, for there is some fine float fishing on the upper part of this run in the late spring and early summer months. When we drifted here, the surface was an almost continual eruption of trout, steelhead, and salmon, ranging from pan-sized up to 4 pounders. The water here is crystal clear and cold enough to keep the game fish very spirited.

There are only four or five riffles between the put-in and Clements bridge, 6 miles downstream, the first take-out point for float fishermen. But the current moves well and the riverbanks are busy with foliage and bird life. The take-out at Clements, if you prefer just this very short run, is on the left shore, alongside the bridge abutment. There is a good carry-out road, connecting with Highway 88, on the downstream side of the bridge.

Most boaters will want to continue on to either Lockeford, another 6 miles downstream, or Victor, 5 miles downstream of Lockeford. The gradient tapers off to almost flat water on this portion of the run, with just enough riffles to make it enjoyable as a first moving-water experience. There are no major obstacles, although shallow water may be a problem in later summer. This run is also popular with experienced boaters who enjoy the solitude and lazy peace of slower water and pleasant swimming holes.

The take-out at the Lockeford bridge is best on the left bank and downstream edge for the carry-out to Elliott Road and the 1-mile trip into Lockeford. There is also carry-out access on the numerous frontage roads not far from the riverbank at Victor. This small town is less than half a mile from the riverbank, and a number of riverside residences marks its location for boaters.

The Mokelumne retains a Class I character all the way from Victor to its confluence with the Consumnes River at Thornton— about 24 miles of meandering valley stream flanked with willows and oak and featuring a major egret and heron rookery near the confluence. There are bridge crossings for take-outs at Highway 50, 4 miles from Victor, at Woodbridge, 6½ miles from Victor, and then at the end on the left and downstream side of the Galt–Thornton bridge. This final section from Victor is a full day's run in canoe, as the current slows to a very leisurely pace. The "Lodi" quadrangle can be used on this run. Like most other valley streams, the Mokelumne tends to lose much of its otherwise peaceful appeal in the hot summer and fall months, when the low water isn't able to handle all of the wastes pouring into it along the way.

The Stanislaus River
(46 miles · CLASS II–IV)

MORE than a thousand square miles of some of the state's most picturesque mountain country make up the drainage basin of the 100-mile-long Stanislaus River, but the guide comments are limited to the fast-disappearing boatable sections. It originates at the crest of the High Sierra, 10,000 feet above sea level. Forty miles from its headwaters, the prime tributaries, the North and Middle Forks, come together. Six miles downstream, above Columbia, the smaller South Fork joins in.

Once the sight of feverish gold panning, the Stanislaus has more recently been raped for its hydroelectric wealth. The triumvirate of PG&E and the Oakdale and South San Joaquin Irrigation districts have built four dams along the once pristine and cascading river, and a massive fifth one—the New Melones Dam—will soon be under construction.

The hydroelectric and diversion works have returned one small consolation for the havoc they have wreaked on the natural river. They deliver a sustained boatable flow throughout most of the year after the spring flood runout. But what PG&E giveth with one hand, it and the federal government can—and will—take away with the other. The New Melones Dam, which is planned for completion in 1978, will bury the river's last piece of quality white water, despite the protest of environmentalists and sportsmen. Although the decision is irreversible, we offer a description of the run here in the hope it will attract more boaters and, hopefully, more members of the campaign to stem other pointless and destructive dams.

The Stanislaus River is a sporty Class I-II for nearly
7 miles between Parrot's Ferry and Highway 49,
stretches like this drawing canoe, kayak or rafts.

PG&E Camp 9 to Parrot's Ferry
(10 miles • CLASS IV • *Running Time 3 hours)*
USGS 15 minute quadrangle map *"Columbia"*

• This upper run of the Stanislaus starts just below the regulating dam south of Avery off Highway 4 and is the busiest and most popular white water left in the state. While it is in use most of the year because of the controlled flow, only a scant few dare the rigors of the numbing cold water and the biting temperature of winter. The Stanislaus can be dangerous during spring flood and it should be upgraded to a Class V here because of the powerful surge of the current. Only experts should ply this section during high water.

The first 5 miles below the launching site, at Camp No. 9 downstream of the last regulating dam, are the toughest as the river plummets through a steep, rocky gorge and over a series of thrilling drops and rapids pocked with very high waves. While only a modest challenge to the big commercial rafts, these combers provide amateurs and kayak and decked-canoe paddlers with some highly prized white-water running. At least three professional rafting firms run customers over this scenic piece of river.

The river picks up both bulk and speed with the addition of the Middle Fork, 3 miles above the put-in, and the smaller South Fork just before the take-out at Parrot's Ferry. Craft will find a take-out on the left side of the river, just downstream of the Parrot's Ferry bridge, in a small pool. This spot also serves as the put-in for the succeeding and easier section.

Parrot's Ferry to Highway 49
(6.5 miles • CLASS II–III • *Running Time 2½ hours)*
USGS 15-minute quadrangle map *"Columbia"*

• This pleasant run through an isolated river canyon is reached by taking the Columbia park turnoff from Highway 49, just a few miles north of Sonora. In this Mother Lode country, a a gold pan should be part of every boater's duffle. Though the chances of a strike are slim, even when scratching out deep

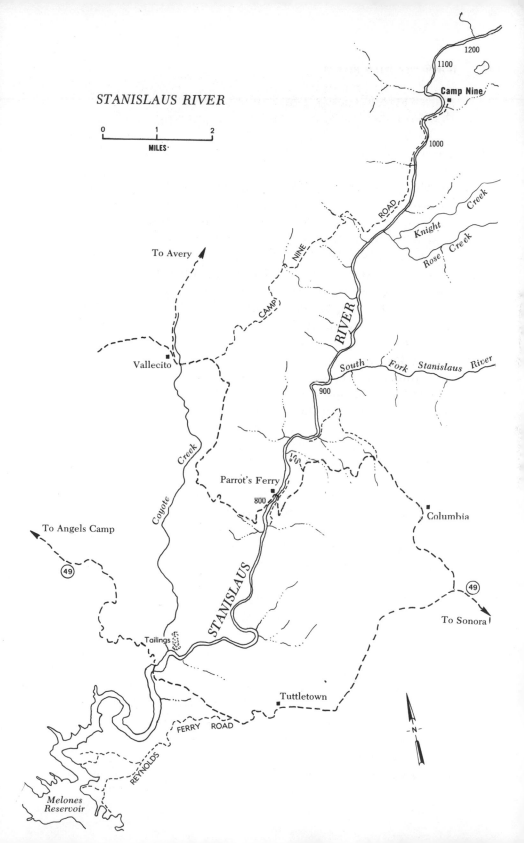

STANISLAUS RIVER

0   1   2
MILES

1200
1100
Camp Nine
1000

Knight Creek
Rose Creek

ROAD

RIVER

CAMP NINE

To Avery

South Fork Stanislaus River

900

Vallecito

Creek

Parrot's Ferry

800

Coyote

To Angels Camp

Columbia

49

49

To Sonora

STANISLAUS

Tailings

Tuttletown

N

FERRY ROAD

REYNOLDS

Melones Reservoir

underwater crevices, there is an excitement and thrill just from the effort that makes it every bit worthwhile.

The launch spot for the Stanislaus is reached by a narrow, paved road on the south side of the canyon, 200 yards uphill from the aging and narrow one-way bridge that replaced the historic ferry first used by John C. Fremont in 1844. From the parking area, enter the upper end of the quiet pool just below the bridge. There is a small, bouncy rapid right below this pool that will get the trip off to an exciting start.

There are only two Class III rapids on this run, the first about a mile downstream and the other another mile and a half further down. In between are a series of rollicking, frothy Class IIs, separated by deep, crystal-clear pools that become a favorite holding and feeding spot for trout when the Melones Reservoir heats up too much in summer.

The last 2½ miles of the stretch to the Highway 49 bridge are comparatively flat water, depending, of course, on the time of year and the water flow. Early in the spring, when the reservoir is very low and the river quite high, the whole run should be upgraded at least one notch to Class III-IV. And, in April and May, beware of the powerful, surging rapids half a mile upstream of the Highway 49 bridge. At this time of year, they would be a difficult but rewarding run for intermediates and upwards. A similar distance downstream of the bridge, there is another rapids, with a sharp left curve midway down, that is highly prized by good white-water runners.

The run from Parrot's Ferry should not take longer than 2½ hours, even allowing time for emptying the canoe out at least twice because of the strong wave action. The take-out is several hundred yards above the bridge, on the right where there are a number of campsites. This area, because it is grassy and because of the constant fluctuation in the water level, has become a productive breeding ground for mosquitos. Boaters should have the spray or dope ready.

In the spring, before Melones Reservoir is full, and in the late fall, when its level drops considerably, experienced boaters can finish the run all the way to the lake through another 6 or 7 miles of isolated, swift, challenging water. Shuttle-car access for the pick-up is on Reynolds Ferry road, turning west off Highway 49 just north of Tuttletown. The road takes you right down to the lakeshore at the head of the reservoir.

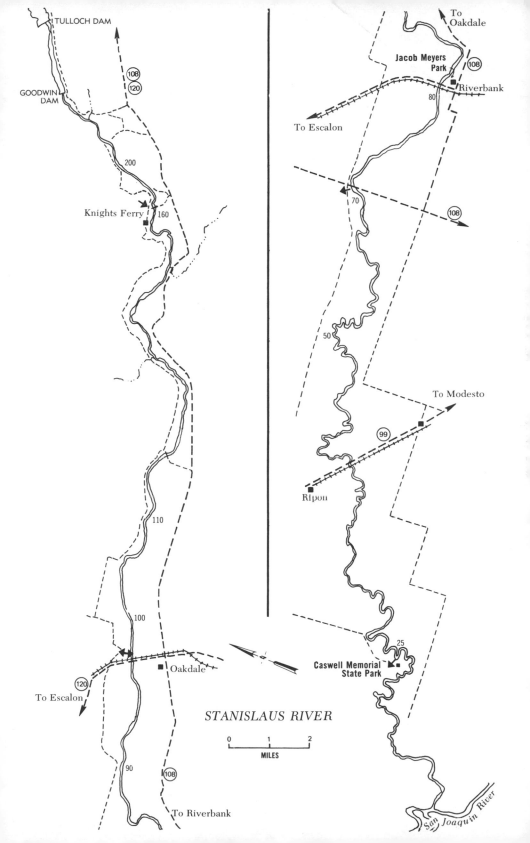

TULLOCH DAM

To Oakdale

Jacob Meyers Park

108

Riverbank

80

GOODWIN DAM

108

120

To Escalon

70

108

200

Knights Ferry 160

50

To Modesto

99

110

Ripon

100

Oakdale

25

120

Caswell Memorial State Park

To Escalon

STANISLAUS RIVER

0   1   2

MILES

90

108

To Riverbank

San Joaquin River

Knight's Ferry to Oakdale
(*18 miles* • CLASS I–II • *Running Time 5½ hours*)
USGS 15 minute quadrangle maps
"Copperopolis" and "Oakdale"

• This is one of the finest open-canoe runs in the state, offering
a perfect mix of easy white water and clear, slow-moving river.
The stretch is ideal for swimming, has good fishing (though fish
are on the small side), and has pretty streamside campsites. While
Knight's Ferry is the first good access point, it might be more
than worthwhile to carry canoes in for the mile it would take
to reach the small gorge downstream from Tullock Dam. There
is no finer scenery nor greater isolation than in this benchland
of the San Joaquin Valley's easy side. The perpendicular cliffs
of brown sandstone are a haven for swallows, hawks, and the
quietly rolling Stanislaus. And the water discreetly retains its
Class I–II character all the way to Knight's Ferry, adding another
3 miles of isolated beauty and easy touring to the run. A residence
about a mile downstream of Tulloch Dam might be able to deliver
more information on foot access to this part of the river.

To reach Knight's Ferry, take that historic town's turnoff from
Highway 120 east of Oakdale. Camera buffs know this road well,
for it leads to a classic covered bridge over the river just east
of the small town. Ideal access to the river is from the Knight's
Ferry Park adjacent to the historical marker on the south side
of the main street.

There is a classic long, swift, and challenging Class II chute
half a mile downstream from the put-in. First-timers should pull
out to the right where the raised ledge begins in order to scout
this run. We had to take the head of the chute slightly to the
right of center in order to miss protruding rocks. Then it was
a case of bearing sharply to the right and staying within a paddle
length of the steep bank for almost 200 yards of exhilarating
chop and swirl.

Beyond, most of the remainder of the run to Oakdale is a
peaceful Class I, with some riffles along the way to keep things
interesting. There are many irrigation diversion works and the
river twists sharply away, and usually to the left, in front of
them. Nearly each of these turns develop quick little riffles that
spice up the run. Rounding one of these corners in the meander-

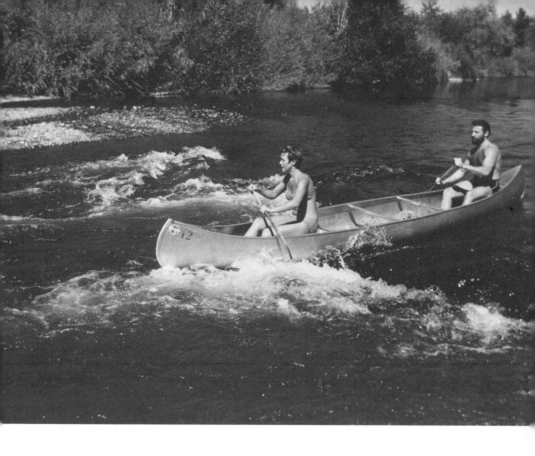

Lower stretches of the Stanislaus include this
scenic region between Knight's Ferry and Oakdale,
an 18-mile run and one of the more picturesque of
the lower Sierra rivers. It is a perfect training run
for beginners.

ing watercourse, we came so close to a rare red fox sunning himself on a hidden sand spit that we could count his rusty whiskers. He didn't twitch or show the faintest signs of fear or surprise as we drifted quietly past. My son and I were so astonished, we didn't so much as utter a sound. Later, it seemed as though there should have been more fanfare, more recognition of such a rare touch of the Old West.

The take-out at Oakdale is on the right bank, just upstream from the Highway 120 bridge. Gear has to be walked up a mildly slanting grade to the frontage road leading to the highway. When traffic isn't too heavy, gear can be shuttled across the road to the parking area.

Oakdale to Highway 36 Bridge
(12 miles • CLASS I • Running Time 4½ hours)
USGS 15 minute quadrangle maps
"Escalon" and "Riverbank"

• The launch spot is the same as the take-out at Oakdale. Beginning here opens up a very peaceful 8-mile run through willows and cottonwoods to the bustling town of Riverbank. This is a perfect place for a mid-day picnic in the peaceful Jacob Meyers Park at the river's edge.

The Highway J6 bridge take-out is another 4 miles downstream, and the classic flat countryside and current remain the same throughout the run. This stretch is an ideal beginner's run in early spring, when the water and weather are still cool and fragrant. Remember that the flatter the valley terrain and the more settled its riverbanks, the less attractive these Sierra rivers will be. Few of them, below this point, are free of the telltale stench of sewage and pesticide. Also, water level becomes a crucial factor beyond mid-May. Even then, the spreading orchard's and other agricultural developments are sucking more and more of the rivers' lifeblood.

The Tuolumne River
(46 miles · CLASS I–IV–V)

FOR open boaters, the Tuolumne is something like the big one that always gets away. Its upper portions—rated some of the finest and most challenging white water in the state—are too tough for them, and the quieter lower segments are virtually inaccessible. A concerted battle is now being waged to open up access to the whole river by getting it placed on the scenic and wild rivers list. What the Sierra Club's Tuolumne River Conference had to say about the river's pristine beauty suggests why so much effort has been devoted to the project:

> The 158-mile long Tuolumne River arises from the Mt. Lyell Glacier in Yosemite National Park and plunges down the western Sierra Nevada to join the San Joaquin River near Modesto. In its brief course, the river has carved one of the major canyons of the world, provides sparkling drinking water to San Francisco customers, offers a magnificent kayaking course, wildlife sanctuary, and fishing area, fills one of the largest reservoirs in California, irrigates and meanders through some of the richest farmland in the world, and provides a significant King salmon spawning environment.

The Sierra Club has been joined by many others in seeking the wild-river designation for the Tuolumne and in blocking construction of any more new dams on the river. In fact, conservationists are demanding the abandonment of the massive O'Shaughnessy Dam, which backs up the notorious Hetch Hetchy Reservoir and the aging Lake Eleanor Dam. They argue that the massive New Don Pedro Dam on the benchland far downstream provides more than enough water-storage capacity to maintain San Francisco's huge delivery system and that it also provides ultimate flood-control protection.

The 18-mile course from Lumsden Campground to Wards Ferry bridge is already being called one of the greatest continuous white-water runs in the country. It is also one of the most beautiful; the water is crystal clear and the deep, isolated canyon is frocked with a magnificent cloak of greenery and wild flowers. At even its lowest water flow, this section of the river rates a Class IV + ranking from veteran white-water boaters. At higher flows, common because of frequent releases of water from Hetch Hetchy, the rating climbs to Class V and even Class VI. All of which explains graphically why it is out of bounds for canoeists. Rafters and kayakers, however, are discovering a priceless new gem in the state's waterways here.

LaGrange Dam to Waterford

(*18 miles* • CLASS I • *Running Time 6 hours*)
USGS 15 minute quadrangle maps
"Merced Falls," "Cooperstown," and "Paulsell"

• It would not be ethical for me to encourage the use of this section of the river, because it involves trespassing both putting in and taking out. However, I wish to describe the run in order to encourage others to demand of their legislators that this and other rivers like it in the state immediately be taken out of the realm of "private plaything" for adjoining landowners.

This is a perfect Class I moving river and a pretty, twisting stream as well. There are exciting but mild riffles throughout the run and drops that even beginners can handle. The current is steady and strong enough to deliver an exciting feel for river running.

I searched in vain to locate the owner of property flanking the narrow one-way LaGrange-Keystone bridge, north out of LaGrange on Highway J59. Then we climbed over the fence at the bridge and put-in there to complete a perfectly beautiful run. One of the most endearing qualities of this section of the Tuolumne is the breathtaking heron and snowy egret rookeries in the gigantic oak trees along the south bank, 10 miles from the put-in.

About 12 miles downstream, we again had a run-in with the hateful barbed wire some ranchers feel they have a right to string across a public, navigable waterway. We had to duck low in our boat once and quickly pull to shore another time to avoid the menacing blockades across the entire stream.

The take-out is at the second bridge crossing, where the Hickman–Waterford road to Highway 132 leads back to LaGrange.

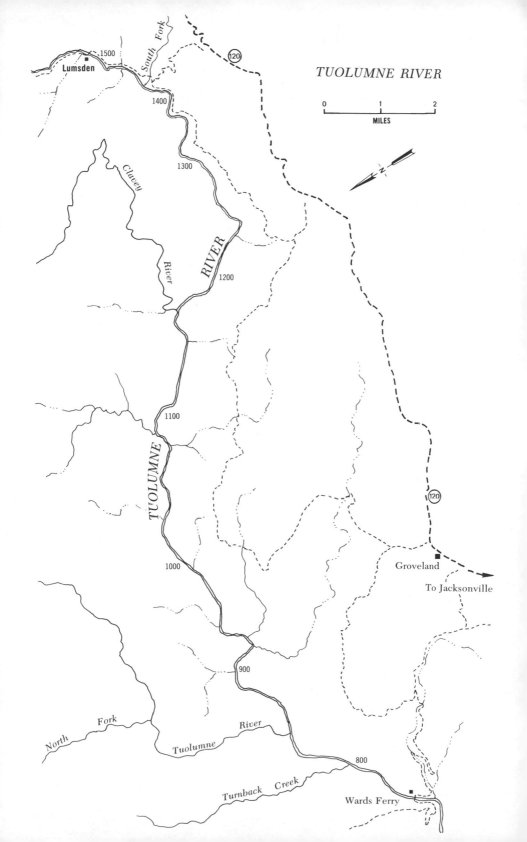

TUOLUMNE RIVER

Lumsden
1500
South Fork
120
1400
1300
Clavey
River
RIVER
1200
1100
TUOLUMNE
1000
120
Groveland
To Jacksonville
900
North Fork
Tuolumne River
Turnback Creek
Wards Ferry
800

0   1   2
MILES

Sacramento Valley and Coastal Rivers

The Feather River
(*90 miles* · CLASS I)

A LUSTY novel or a fascinating historical book could be written on this single river, so strongly is its story woven into the state's colorful past. Once one of the prime northern Sierra boating streams, the Feather River's best running section has been flooded by the gigantic Oroville Reservoir. Its original name, El Rio de las Plumas (River of the Feathers), hardly describes its lower sections now. But boaters have learned to take the bitter with the sweet. At least the giant Oroville project has opened up a year-round, 50-mile course of relatively flat, moving water that is a fine stretch for beginners or lazy paddlers. Upstream from Oroville, the water is still wild and mostly impassable.

Oroville Dam to Sacramento
(*50 miles* · CLASS I · *Running Time 9 hours*)
USGS 15-minute quadrangle maps
"Gridley," "Marysville," and "Knights Landing"

• The current on the Feather River is steady through most of the year, and there are very few tough rapids from the base of the dam all the way to the take-out point, the Yuba City marina, just downstream of the second bridge in Yuba City. There is put-in access at the Oroville marina, which is on the dam road just off the Oroville–Feather Falls Road.

Most of the Feather River run is well-isolated, though it flows through productive farmland and there are any number of rough, stream-side campsites along the way. The more adventurous types may want to experience the physical challenge of running the Feather the full 90 miles all the way to its confluence with the Sacramento. While this additional 40 miles is not particularly scenic or challenging, it can be a rather unique experience to run this distance on flat, fairly swift-moving water.

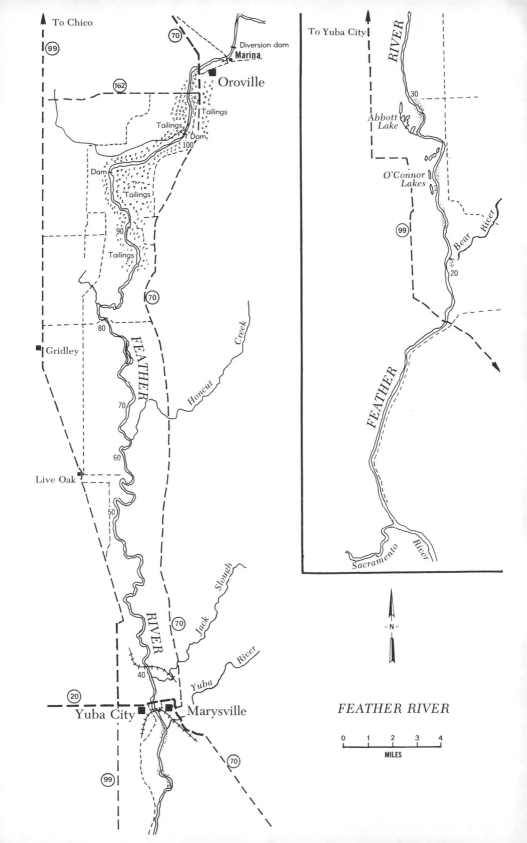

FEATHER RIVER

0 1 2 3 4
MILES

The Sacramento River
(*148 miles* • CLASS I–IV)

ONCE called the "Nile of the West," this vast waterway carries nearly one third of the total annual runoff from all California streams—22 million acre-feet—from its headwaters in a small lake on Mount Eddy in the Klamath Range to its mouth in Suisun Bay, 50 miles from San Francisco. That's more water than the mighty Colorado carries. Not all of it stays in the riverbed. Nearly 4 million acre-feet is siphoned off along the way for domestic, industrial, and agricultural use, much of it routed to the thirsty Southland through the California Aqueduct. Greedy water companies covetously eye the remainder of the flow and plan for diversions that could ultimately cut the yearly flow more than in half.

As disastrous as that might be ecologically, boaters draw solace from the fact that most of the diversion will come near the mouth of the river, guaranteeing them a continuing year-round waterway. The mighty Sacramento is not so much like a river anymore as it is a giant canal, at least downstream from the double breastworks that are Shasta and Keswick dams above Redding. Most of the year it runs almost bank-full, carrying billions of gallons of pure Shasta water to the parched and glutted Southland. From Redding to Sacramento, this "canal" offers boaters 125 miles of virtually flat, fast-moving water that is an ideal glide for beginners and a nice easy change of pace for the experienced paddler.

The 43 miles of wild river above the still waters of Shasta are too demanding for open canoes, but they are highly prized for kayaks, decked canoes, and rafting. The landscape in this headwater drainage through canyons of lava rock is rugged, and its lower slopes are heavily wooded. Below Keswick Dam, however, the river gives an impression not unlike the Amazon—a wide, powerful river flanked by heavy forests and cut off from the outside world. Of course, the forest belt is only a matter of a few yards wide, and the outside world is sometimes so near

An upstream look at the Sacramento River, just below Redding, shows big thunderheads building over snow-tipped Mt. Shasta. This run of swift but flat water is becoming more popular each year.

that swanky riverside homes often hove into view. But even the houses are beautiful in this setting and do little to spoil the mood of "jungle" isolation. Mt. Shasta, with its sparkling crest of snow, towers over the headwaters of the river; and, at times, the Trinity Alps and the High Sierra are easily visible to the west and east.

Box Canyon Dam to Shasta Retreat
(*8 miles* • CLASS IV • *Running Time 6 hours*)
USGS 15 minute quadrangle map *"Weed"*

• This section of the Sacramento, as the rating indicates, is not meant for open canoes. Nor is it meant for beginners in even the most sturdy of watertight craft. While the scenery through this deep canyon run is entrancing, only advanced intermediate boaters will be safe here. The gradient is consistently steep, mostly between 75 and 100 feet per mile, with a swift flow, very cold water, and some extremely sharp drops. It is, however, an exciting challenge for advanced white-water hands. The run often takes as long as 6 hours to negotiate because of the many scouting stops required. Along this twisting waterway is the storied Mossbrae Falls, where incoming springs well up from lava ridges above and trickle over the thick moss beds to form a magical water curtain along the undercut bank below. About 100 yards long, the falls can be run, or it can be bypassed on the outside of the undercut bank.

Shasta Retreat to Dog Creek
(*30 miles* • CLASS IV • *Running Time 14 hours*)
USGS 15 minute quadrangle maps
"Dunsmuir" and "Lamoine"

• There are only a few short Class III stretches here. Most of this run is swift and demanding Class IV, not suitable at all for open canoes. The run is quite popular with kayakers, however, because of its fairly stable year-round flow. Trout fishing in this area is another drawing card, although the fish are not very large and the natural fishery is now supported more each year by the state stocking program of hatchery-raised fish.

There are several miles of water below Dog Creek that are sometimes run in late summer and fall as the water level of

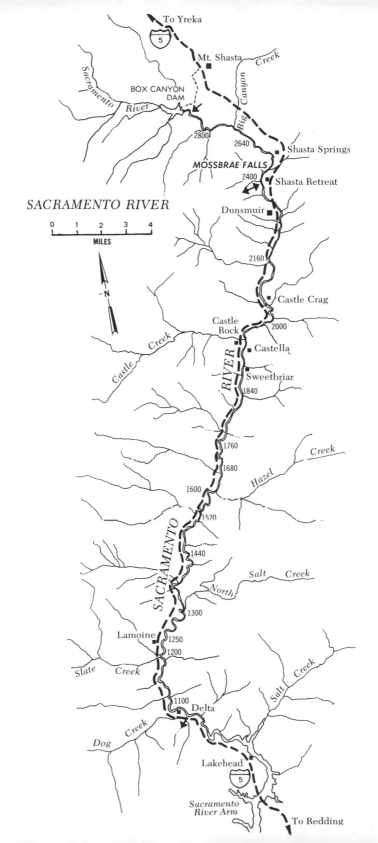

To Yreka

5

Mt. Shasta

BOX CANYON
DAM

Sacramento

River

2800

Big *Canyon*

Creek

2640

Shasta Springs

MOSSBRAE FALLS

2400

Shasta Retreat

SACRAMENTO RIVER

Dunsmuir

| 0 | 1 | 2 | 3 | 4 |

MILES

2160

–N–

Castle Crag

2000

Castle
Rock

RIVER

Castella

Castle

Creek

Sweetbriar

1840

1760

Creek

1680

Hazel

1600

1520

SACRAMENTO

1440

Salt *Creek*

North

1300

Lamoine

1250

1200

Slate *Creek*

Salt *Creek*

1100

Delta

Dog *Creek*

Lakehead

5

Sacramento
River Arm

To Redding

Lake Shasta drops. In the spring and summer, though, when the lake is building up full, this stretch is mostly calm water and a demanding paddle that is seldom tackled.

Redding to Ball's Ferry
(22 miles • CLASS I–II • *Running Time 4 hours)*
USGS 15 minute quadrangle maps
"Redding," "Anderson," and "Tucson Buttes"

• The run from Redding to Ball's Ferry in early July can be a delight. It can be run from the base of Keswick Dam, 3 miles upriver from Redding, or from the city lagoon at the south end of Redding, reached by Marina Drive off of Highway 44. The Keswick put-in is reached from the last Redding off-ramp from Interstate 5. Turn right at the main street intersection in town and follow the old highway north across the river to Keswick Dam road, just across the river and to the left. Once on the way downstream from Keswick, care must be taken to avoid the small diversion dam just upstream from the main bridge in Redding. Boaters should pull out on the left shore 100 yards above the obvious drop. The portage is short and easy.

From there, the river snakes through town without any challenging water until you reach the south end of the city, opposite the large concrete civic auditorium on the right bank. The river splits around an island and the best passage is closest to the banks on either fork. Both are marked with high, exciting waves, but the passages are wide and relatively free of obstructions. The water is rough and pocked with boulders between these passages, however. The optional put-in at the city lagoon below bypasses these sections and is a safer route for beginners.

The river is very wide and swift at this point—between 7 and 8 miles an hour. Beyond the first long stretch near the auditorium, there are a few more exciting but considerably easier runs, requiring only an occasional stroke to keep the bow heading into the white water. Snow-capped peaks rise in the distance, and swallows flit out of their little mud-hut nests beneath the four bridges that span the Sacramento between the Redding auditorium and the Ball's Ferry bridge take-out. Palatial riverside homes, set in the center of sweeping emerald-green lawns and shaded by huge black oaks and weeping willows, add a not-unpleasant dimension to the ride.

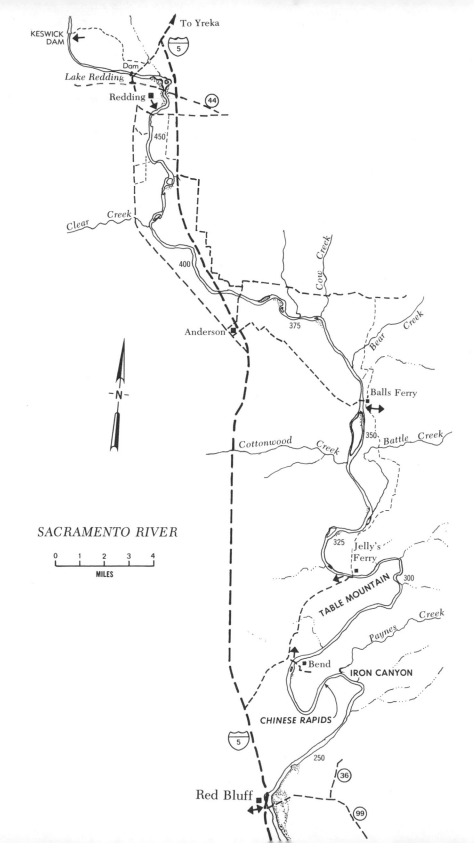

KESWICK
DAM

To Yreka

⑤

Dam

Lake Redding

Redding

㊹

450

Clear   Creek

400

Cow Creek

Anderson

375

Bear   Creek

Balls Ferry

350   *Battle   Creek*

Cottonwood   Creek

SACRAMENTO RIVER

0   1   2   3   4
MILES

325   Jelly's
Ferry

300

TABLE MOUNTAIN

Paynes   Creek

■ Bend

IRON CANYON

CHINESE RAPIDS

⑤

250

㊱

Red Bluff

㊲

About 7 miles downstream from Redding, near a major sand and gravel quarry operation on the right bank, there are two sizable spits that offer enough willow cover for privacy should anyone prefer breaking the run for an overnight camp.

The splendid tree-lined stretch on to Ball's Ferry is a favorite with anglers. Besides the annual steelhead and salmon runs in the fall and early winter months, there is productive fishing for native trout of up to 4 pounds. Their bigger migrant cousins in the area often weigh up to five times that. The trick in fishing in these waters is to work the river and its pockets back and forth, with a trolling speed just fast enough to impede your otherwise rapid drift downstream. Lures, worms, roe, and flies all work well here.

The fourth bridge signals Ball's Ferry, and at the left bank, about 150 yards downstream of the bridge piles, there is a shaded cove leading to a launching ramp. The ramp turn-in is marked by an outcropping of rusty brown jetty rocks just above the waterline. Ball's Ferry County Park, a quarter of a mile up the road, offers fire pits, camp toilets, running water, a fresh well-cropped lawn, and scores of large oak shade trees for hot and weary campers.

The only obstacles during this 22-mile glide are the auditorium rapids and the abutments of the four bridges, some of which trap large snarls of driftwood and create tough undercurrents and sucking eddies. In almost every case, though, the river is wide enough to permit the more cautious and inexperienced boater plenty of room to draw clear to calmer water.

Ball's Ferry to Red Bluff
(*34 miles* • CLASS I–II • *Running Time 7½ hours*)
USGS 15 minute quadrangle maps
"Tucson Buttes" and "Red Bluff"

• The descent of the river slows noticeably along this portion of the valley, even though the riverbed cuts though a gorge bounded by high bluffs. While the current is still a most helpful ally on this run, more paddling is needed than on the Redding-Ball's Ferry section. Only two obstacles along this route are worth mentioning. One is about 5 miles downstream from Ball's Ferry, where the roar of fast water sounds much worse than it later

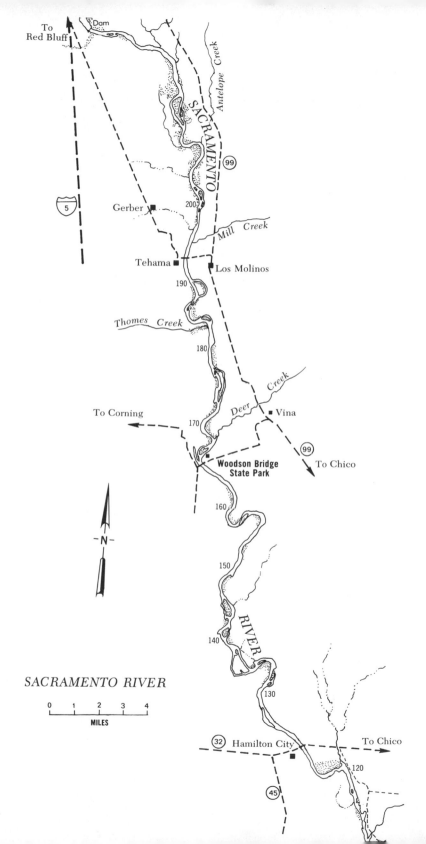

To
Red Bluff

Dam

Antelope Creek

SACRAMENTO

99

5

Gerber

200

Mill Creek

Tehama

Los Molinos

190

Thomes Creek

180

Deer Creek

Vina

To Corning

170

99

Woodson Bridge
State Park

To Chico

160

150

RIVER

140

SACRAMENTO RIVER

130

0 1 2 3 4
MILES

-N-

32 Hamilton City

To Chico

45

120

proves to be. Here, the river slams into a high, almost perpendicular cliff on the left, creating one of the biggest back-boils or underslicks we have ever seen. It does not, however, classify as a whirlpool, though it is sometimes called that by locals. So long as the boater keeps his balance and offsets the odd current reversals with sweeping draw-strokes off the bow, there is little to fear. Bearing slightly left of the river's center line here will help you bypass the worst of the slick. The upwelling is from the combination of a large back-eddy from the cliff and a deep reversal from the undercurrent sweeping upward out of a deep hole gouged in the riverbed.

The first crossing and access point, Jelly's Ferry, is about 10 miles short of Red Bluff and 5 miles above the next access point, Bend Ferry. Both points are reached by a well-marked Jelly's Ferry Road off-ramp from Interstate 5, 8 miles north of Red Bluff. The road to Bend Ferry is 6 miles and Jelly's Ferry is 3 miles further up. Both crossings are accessible for take-outs on the right bank and the upstream sides of the bridges. The Red Bluff take-out is near the boat-launching ramp on the right bank, nor far below the center of town.

The other major obstacle is the historic Chinese Rapids, just before Red Bluff. The Chinese Rapids cut through one of the several lava rock ridges that flank the river in this area. Both above and below the rapids are favored resting holes for steelhead and salmon when the runs are on. The wave action through that stretch is significant enough to break the tedium of the coasting ride the rest of the river offers and please the experienced paddler. Although the run is rated Class II, it is safe for trained beginners in open canoes. For the others of less capability, there is sufficient room to draw clear of the rough water.

Camping on this entire stretch is fairly limited, since the full river offers precious few sand or gravel bars. One that we highly recommend is at the mouth of Cottonwood Creek, just a few miles downstream and on the right from Ball's Ferry. In spring and early summer, this site offers warm enough water for a pleasant swim and fair trout fishing. There are also a few other good campsites on the west bank another 5 miles further down the Sacramento.

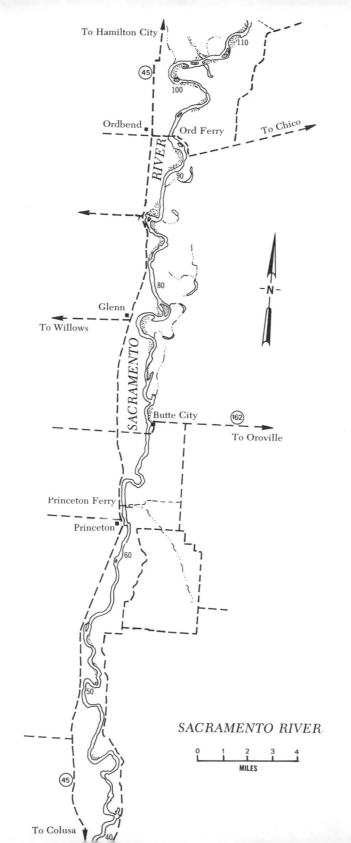

To Hamilton City

45

110

100

Ordbend

Ord Ferry

To Chico

RIVER

90

-N-

80

Glenn

To Willows

SACRAMENTO

Butte City

162

To Oroville

Princeton Ferry

Princeton

60

50

SACRAMENTO RIVER

0 1 2 3 4

MILES

45

To Colusa

40

Red Bluff to Knight's Landing
(*72 miles* • CLASS I • *Running Time 18 hours*)
USGS 15 minute quadrangle maps
*"Red Bluff," "Corning," "Chico," "Butte City," "Maxwell,"
"Colusa," "Sutter Buttes," "Dunnigan," and "Knights Landing"*

• This section is ideal for the whole range of watercraft. In fact, you will sight everything from innertubes to big multi-passenger pontoon rafts on this part of the Sacramento. There are a succession of small towns for resupply and take-out, including, in order, Tehama, just below Mill Creek, Woodson Bridge State Park, at Deer Creek, Hamilton City, Glenn, and Butte City. This route divides into a comfortable 45-mile overnighter, thanks to the steady current here that makes a 20-mile day fairly easy. The only obstruction is a diversion dam a mile below Red Bluff that needs a short, easy portage.

The next most likely route, though there are many possible selections here, is from Butte City down through Colusa, Meridian, Cranmore, Kirkville, and Knight's Landing—37 more easy miles. That run can be stretched another 19 miles right into Sacramento, but river traffic is much busier there and it is less scenic. The best take-out on this route, though there are several options, would be at Discovery Park near where the American River flows in from the left.

The Yuba River
(20 miles • CLASS I)

Highway 20 to Marysville
(20 miles • CLASS I *• Running Time 5 hours)*
USGS 15 minute quadrangle maps
"Wheatland" and "Marysville"

• The serene 20-mile stretch along the Yuba from Highway 20 to Marysville may not be one of the most scenic runs in the state, but it is ideal for beginners because of its flat, moving water, plus plenty of elbow room for corrective action when needed. Like any other stream, the Yuba can be run with a variety of speeds, making it a leisurely overnight jaunt—with a halfway camp spot at De Guerre Point Dam—or a more vigorous full day's undertaking all the way to Marysville or Yuba City. While 20 miles sounds like a long day's pull, the spring and early summer current maintains a fairly consistent 5 or 6 miles an hour. At that speed, only a minimum amount of paddling is necessary.

The most popular put-in for this run is at Parks Bar, where Highway 20 crosses the Yuba about 20 miles east of Marysville. Access to the big river bar stretching along below the bridge is gained from a turnout on the south side of the highway, half a mile west of the bridge. Only a short carry is needed to get to the water's edge.

Only a few obstacles are worthy of mention. There is a small rapids encountered at the base of the bar, just a few hundred yards from where the best launching spots are. Beginners should quarter quickly across the stream to skirt its comparatively smooth south edge. Shallower-draft kayaks could easily negotiate the more bouncy white water without getting hung up on the huge boulders just inches beneath the surface on the right. Even experienced open canoeists would be wise to flare slightly to the slick's left side.

De Guerre Dam is easily visible. The gently rolling hills, dotted with a variety of oak and the occasional cottonwood, slant downward on both sides to accentuate the dam's concrete foundations. Most visible is the steep bank rising high above the dam on the right. Boaters should approach the bank on the far left shore and, depending upon the flow, hug the shoreline all the way to the lip of the dam, staying close enough to vault out to shore if there is any feeling of being swept toward the brink. Even when the release from Bridgeport Dam, 6 miles upstream from the Highway 20 bridge, had the river running fairly high and swift, we had no trouble skirting this side and turning sharply to the left back into a mild backwater just near the dam's lip. The portage from here is only several hundred yards up and over the dam.

The rapids below the dam are not to be trifled with. They are a major obstacle to beginners, though a flat easy portage is readily available along the bar. The shallow water is pocked with sub-surface boulders that could make open canoe work most demanding. We ran the center of the stretch for the first 25 yards, skirting the obvious protuberances, and then slashed swiftly over to the far left bank for a shallow but safe chute to the willows' edge and the fast but smooth water below.

Five miles further downstream, there is a long shallow gravel bar jutting out into the river from the left bank. It is not more than a mile and a half below the popular shad holes at the Baldwin Avenue access, where anglers line both shores and make boaters feel as though they are running a modern-day gauntlet of fishing hooks. Here, attracted by continuous splashing in the shallows, we beached and then, delighted with one of the wonders of nature, watched in respectful amazement as hundreds of shad whipped their way up a dozen small channels in the bar to spawn. The golden-finned females would thrash furiously with their tails to scoop out a small bed for the eggs, ease back over the nest to jettison their precious cargo, and then veer off to make room for the male to fin up and spread his milky sperm over the eggs.

Beyond the Baldwim Avenue access and the spawning beds which gave us so much pleasure, stands of stately cottonwoods predominate, flanking the river with a dense canopy of green. The flow slows noticeably and the river deepens for a more restful downhill course.

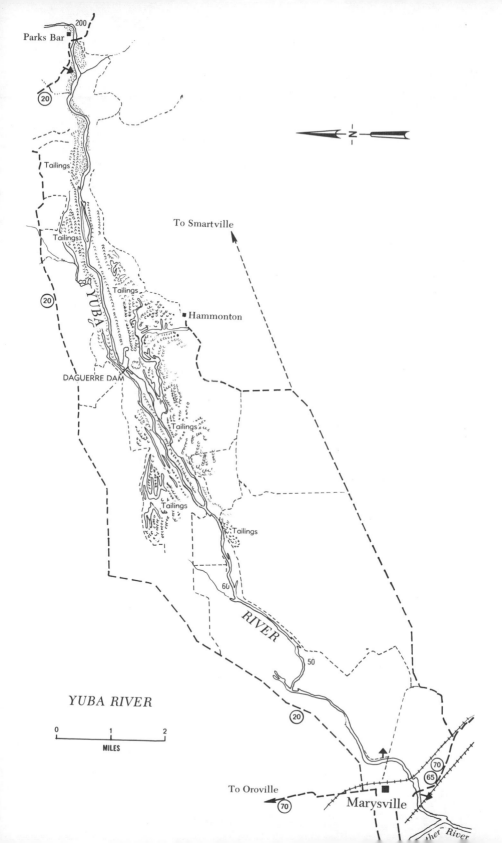

Parks Bar

200

20

Tailings

Tailings

N

To Smartville

YUBA

Tailings

20

Hammonton

DAGUERRE DAM

Tailings

Tailings

Tailings

Tailings

60

RIVER

50

YUBA RIVER

0   1   2
MILES

20

70

65

To Oroville

70

Marysville

ther River

Prime take-outs are to the left side of the first highway bridge, where a river frontage road is just 10 yards above the bank, or a mile further downstream, where a massive sand and gravel bar stretches out beneath the Highway 99 bridge. More ambitious boaters can continue on another mile and a half downriver to the confluence with the Feather River. Crossing over the Feather, there is prime shuttle car access on the far shore.

Touring on the Yuba will be as attractive as your outlook allows. If you're thinking negatively, you will see the ugliness of the huge gravel spoil piles left by the greedy gold dredges and flanking most of the upper half of the run. You will also despair at the intrusion of noisy military jets from Beale Air Force Base, on the upper portion of the river. However, those grotesque banks cry out with history, relics of days in California's past that are worth remembering. Furthermore, the water of the Yuba is crystal clear on this run. And, finally, one of the real thrills for an early June boater is that of watching the vast schools of migrating shad heading upriver to spawn. If you're a fisherman, you will be cheered by the fact that it is not unusual to hook as many as 50 fish in a day during the season. Those who get as much of a thrill merely seeing nature in action can watch the shad migrate up fish ladders at either side of the dam, a low-level diversion project.

The Salmon River

(48 miles • CLASS II–IV)

THE Salmon River has not been well scouted and, as a result, it has not yet come into popularity with boaters. However, it has some very interesting possibilities. In fact, judging from the scenic beauty and the running quality of the 21½-mile stretch from the Forks of The Salmon to the juncture with the Klamath, one could say that the Salmon might be one of the prime pieces of white water in the north end of the state. This beautiful stream has a fairly prolonged boating season, from spring through late summer for prime-time paddlers, and it offers an abundance of visual benefits to the wildlife and scenery buffs.

The Salmon's headwaters are a scattering of tiny lakes in the Marble Mountain Wilderness Area for the North Fork, which tumbles downward 2,400 feet in the first 5½ miles from English Lake. The South Fork rises from a glacier bed on 9,000-foot-high Thompson Peak in the Trinity Alps, picking up a score of feeder streams off the east slope of the Salmon Mountains.

NORTH FORK

Idlewild Campground to Forks of Salmon
(22 miles • CLASS III–IV • *Running Time 8 hours)*
USGS 15-minute quadrangle map *"Sawyers Bar"*

• The put-in, where the Idlewild Campground Road crosses the North Fork about 6 miles above Sawyers Bar, marks the extreme upper boating limits of this smaller of the two main forks—and then only for kayaks, one-man whitewater canoes, and small rafts in early spring. The launch site is reached via the North Fork Road from Forks of Salmon Road off Highway

96 just below Somesbar. Later in the season, put-ins may have to be made from Sawyers Bar to pick up the added flow of Russian Creek and the East Fork.

Gradient patterns through this heavily forested and rocky canyon vary from 45 feet per mile for the first 3 miles below the Idlewild launch to 75 feet per mile from there to Sawyers Bar. The next 5 miles slow down to 36 feet per mile but then pitch into a steep canyon for the next 11 miles to the junction with the South Fork, dropping at a rate of 66 feet to the mile. This whole section is marked by tight-corner maneuvering, some very sharp but only moderately high drops, and plenty of mid-stream rocks.

SOUTH FORK

East Fork Forest Camp to Forks of Salmon
(*27½ miles* • CLASS III–V • *Running Time 9 hours*)
USGS 15 minute quadrangle map *"Cecilville"*

• This larger arm of the river flows a more gradual course. The camp is reached by taking the South Fork Road to 2½ miles beyond the small settlement of Cecilville. This also is the upper boating limit, and the put-in site is actually from the smaller East Fork just a few hundred feet above where it joins the main tributary.

While the general gradient from here to Forks of Salmon averages only 40 feet per mile, there are several short stretches where it reaches 90 feet and 75 feet, plummeting over sharp drops. Some areas here, between Horse Creek and Matthews Creek and between French Creek and the cable crossing below Plummer Creek, may have to be portaged. From Cecilville to Horse Creek, however, the average descent is 32 feet per mile. The take-out is on Acorn Springs Flat, on the left and downstream side of the main river just below the junction with the North Fork. The dirt access road leads back up to the paved South Fork road.

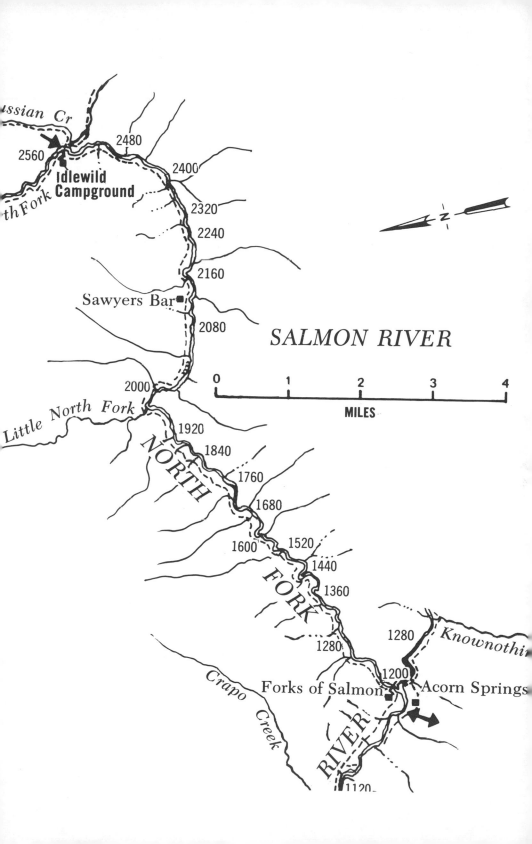

MAIN SALMON

Forks of Salmon to Oak Bottom Campground
(18½ miles • CLASS II–IV • *Running Time 6 hours)*
USGS 15 minute quadrangle map *"Forks of Salmon"*

• With the added water flow from both forks, the Salmon is truly a prized white water stream from the confluence of its main forks to the Klamath. Open canoes, manned by experienced paddlers, can move onto the river here as the gradient slows to an average 34 feet per mile. Access is gained by walking boats down from the main Forks of Salmon Road at the tiny group of cabins or by looping upstream on the South Fork Road and turning back downriver just beyond the bridge.

The first 7 miles of running is through a pleasant but small streamside valley, and the gradient is 22 feet per mile. As the valley funnels into a steep-walled canyon and hooks around Butler Mountain in an exaggerated "heel," the river quickens its pace to 47 feet per mile for the next 8½ miles to Murderers Bar. Throughout this section, the Salmon twists in and out of a series of beautiful, deep pools linked together by frothy ribbons of white water. It is an ideal setting for experienced white-water runners, and the fine, paved road offers excellent scouting opportunities.

There are two good take-outs on this run for those who do not want to continue right on to the bigger Klamath River. The first is at Three Dollar Bar, a quarter of a mile downstream of the second Forks of Salmon Road bridge. Pickup cars can reach streamside by turning off the paved road downstream of the bridge just where the old roadbed is bypassed for the new grade and S-curve. Cutting through a high dirt bank, the old road leads to a long, flat abandoned road section which is fine for camper trucks. For the more mobile crews, a rough travel road leads downhill, giving moderately good passage to several rough campsites, one of them snuggled beneath a huge oak tree and an ideal take-out or launching site.

The river is fairly swift here, but the rapids are mostly only Class II, although some could vary a notch either way depending upon the time of year and water flow involved. Maneuvering

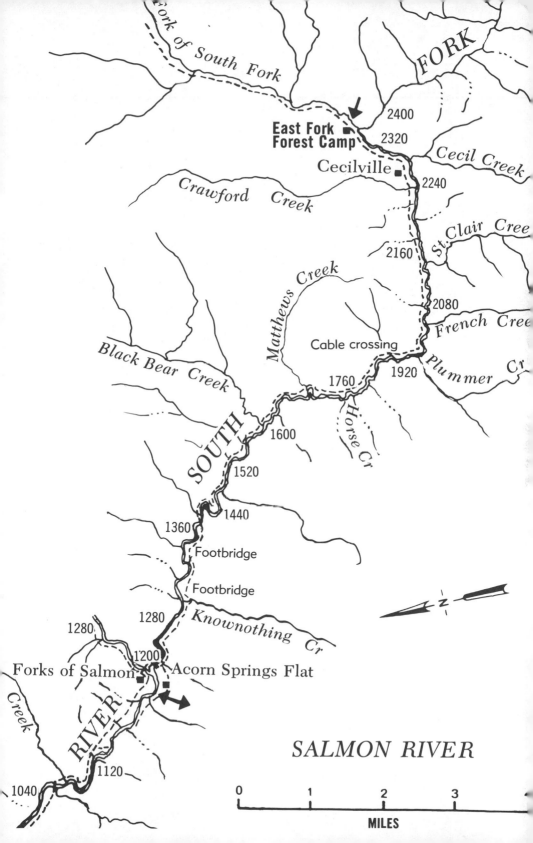

FORK

Fork of South Fork

2400

East Fork
Forest Camp

2320

Cecilville

Cecil Creek

2240

Crawford Creek

St. Clair Creek

2160

Matthews Creek

2080

Cable crossing

French Creek

1760

1920

Plummer Cr

Black Bear Creek

Horse Cr

1600

SOUTH

1520

1440

1360

Footbridge

Footbridge

1280

Knownothing Cr

1280

1200

Forks of Salmon

Acorn Springs Flat

Creek

RIVER

SALMON RIVER

1120

1040

0	1	2	3

MILES

A sharp back eddy caught these boaters on the
Salmon River by surprise, spinning them around
after they shot through the short, bouncy rapid. The
Salmon's short 6-mile course provides ideal access
onto the bigger Klamath River and a prolonged run
for canoe camping.

on fairly sharp corners is the only real test from here down as
you coast through deep canyons to the next and last take-out
before the Klamath, at Oak Bottom campgrounds, 2 miles downstream.

Oak Bottom Campground
to Klamath River
(3 miles · CLASS I–II)

Two dirt roads lead down to this site from Forks of Salmon
Road, one just upstream of the sharp left turn beyond the fire
guard station and the other just at the station. The upper one
is better, leading right to streamside. While this spot serves as
take-out for the previous run, it is more popular as the put-in
for a great combination trip onto the Klamath. Fish are clearly
visible in the clear water and a variety of wildlife scamper
through and along the forested banks and ridges on either side
of the river.

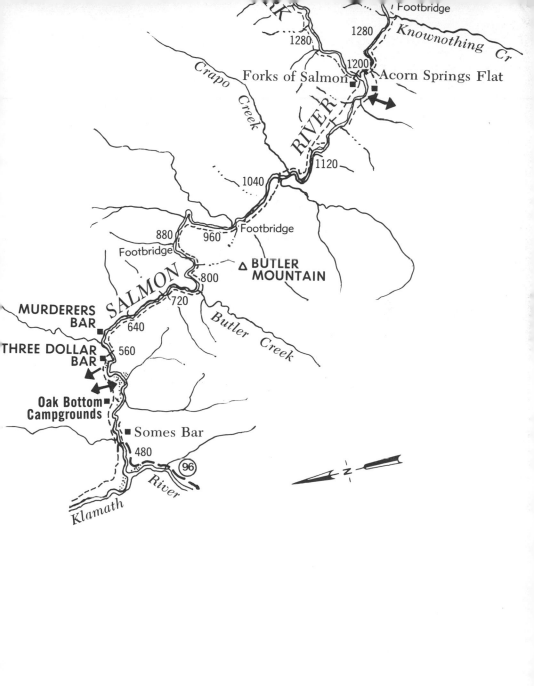

Footbridge

1280   1280   *Knownothing Cr*

Crapo Creek

1200

Forks of Salmon   Acorn Springs Flat

RIVER

1120

1040

880   960   Footbridge

Footbridge

SALMON   800   △ **BUTLER MOUNTAIN**

720

MURDERERS BAR   640   *Butler Creek*

THREE DOLLAR BAR   560

Oak Bottom Campgrounds

■ Somes Bar

480

96

River

Klamath

N

SALMON RIVER

0   1   2   3   4

MILES

The Scott River
(*34 miles* • CLASS II–V)

THIS narrow, twisting river drains the Scott Bar and Marble Mountain ranges over a 68-mile long watershed and then funnels into the Klamath River just upstream from Hamburg on Highway 96. It is basically a white-water stream with only its last 4 miles suitable or safe for open canoes. Kayaks, decked canoes, and small rafts can negotiate most of the upper stretches, but only if they are manned by advanced boaters. The rugged countryside through which most of the river flows is marked with old gold mine sites and is a more arid and less scenic watershed than that of its larger downriver cousin, the Salmon River. The river is paralled by a good road for scouting.

Fort Jones to Scott Bar
(*28 miles* • CLASS IV–V • *Running Time 10 hours*)
USGS 15 minute quadrangle maps
"Fort Jones" and "Scott Bar"

• The upper 18 miles of the Scott, from historic Fort Jones to Kelsey Creek bridge, is a quiet meadow stream alternating with sharply graduated Class V water where the river careens around the lower battlements of Russell and Anderson peaks. The gradient here drops quickly to 60 feet per mile and then, nearing Kelsey Creek, tumbles downward at 100 feet per mile. It is clearly out of bounds for any but expert paddlers. There are several very tight corners and sudden chutes on this stretch. Most of them require scouting and two drops probably should be portaged.

There is no detectable letup in the remaining 10 miles. Depending upon the flow of the current, which normally ranges between 650 and 1,400 cubic feet per second, the Tompkins Creek to Scott Bar segment funnels through an isolated gorge, with several rapids in the IV and V class. High water would mandate several portages here.

The Scott's rambunctious upper course provides
stiff challenges like these to kayakers, but its lower
sections, near the Klamath, are more suited to
open canoes.

Scott Bar to Klamath River
(4 miles •CLASS II • Running Time 1½ hours)
USGS 15-minute quadrangle map *"Seiad Valley"*

• This short but very scenic stretch can make a most pleasant side trip while running the rich water wonderland circuit of the Klamath and Trinity rivers. Otherwise, it is too short to be of much use to open canoes. Access to the short run is on a narrow paved road turning left off Scott Bar road, at the site of the tiny village of Scott Bar itself. A few hundred yards further on, the road crosses an aging wooden bridge, where there is foot access to the river on the downstream side of the east bank. One hundred yards beyond is a modest turnout on the left side of the road that can be used for parking. Open canoes are cautioned against putting in any higher up the river than Scott Bar.

The run to the Klamath is naturally short, less than an hour, but the paddler is richly rewarded with the scenic beauty of a small canyon through which the river winds back and forth. The river is mostly deep quiet pools, linked by a series of short and bouncy Class II rapids of only modest difficulty. The only real challenge is a mile downstream of the bridge, where the river makes a sharp right turn against a steep bluff. Safe passage is just to the right of the center combers and turbulence, and be sure to compensate for the strong reverse eddy at the base of the run before the current swings left again. Another mile further along is the best rapid on this stretch, a long, solid, Class II that offers an exciting heaving ride. When the water level is low, more care may be needed on this rapid, since it could become a series of steeper and shorter drops. As in the case of the Salmon River, the brief Scott River run can be nicely combined with the Klamath by continuing right on to the predominantly Class II water of the Seiad Valley, a bit more demanding because of the larger flow of the Klamath.

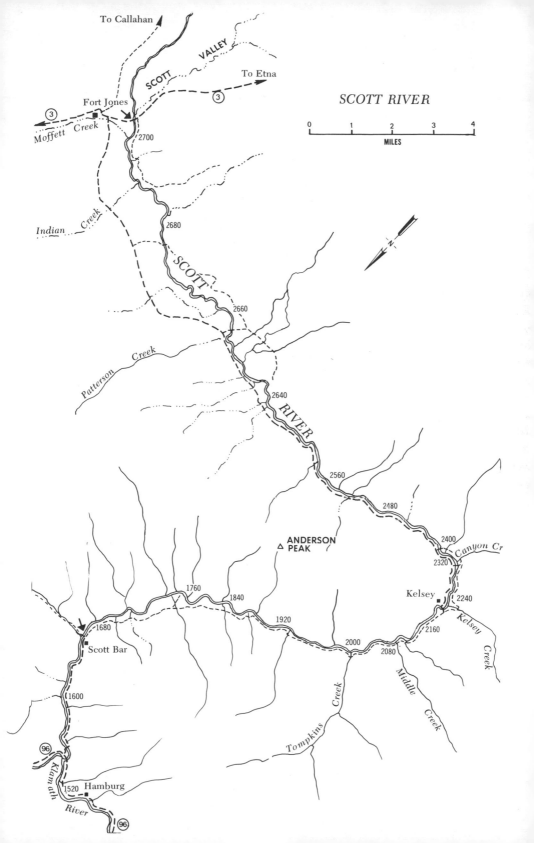

The Big River
(*10 miles* • CLASS I)

WHAT the Big River lacks in size, which is considerable, it more than compensates for in beauty. Its banks are carpeted with ferns and moss. Massive redwoods tower overhead on either side, blotting out the sun. Only the swish of the bow and the whisper of a feathered paddle disrupt the clear blue-green stillness that is magical and serene. From put-in to take-out there is virtually no sign of human life. It is as though you had been caught in a time warp and were back in the frontier days.

Like all of its coastal cousins, the tight corners and twisting course of the Big put a premium on a boater's maneuverability. After heavy rains it can be too hazardous to run, but Boise Cascade Company in Fort Bragg will supply river-condition information by phone as well as grant special weekend permission to use the private roads it maintains in the area of the river. Two weeks after a good rainfall is ideal for a good water level.

Woodlands to Highway 1
(*10 miles* • CLASS I • *Running Time 3 hours*)
USGS 15 minute quadrangle maps
"Comptche" and "Mendocino"

• For ideal launching into the Big River, take the Little Lake road east out of Mendocino on Highway 1 to reach the community of Woodlands, 9 miles inland. At Woodlands, turn right and down to the Boise Cascade Tree Farm.

There is virtually no prolonged chute on the river. It is a small stream that twists around tight corners or floats serenely through small, mist-shrouded meadows. Most of its lower section is a long series of deep holes connected by short, exciting riffles. Trolling or spin casting in the tidal section is productive, though you must be careful about the huge snags trapped in the riverbed. The Big is also a good steelhead stream if you can catch the run.

The best take-out is at the mouth of the river on the north shore, where a road leads down from the north side of the Big River bridge on Highway 1.

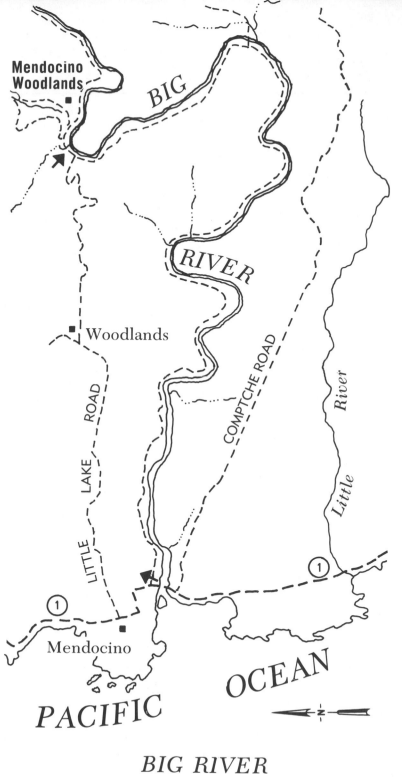

Mendocino Woodlands

Woodlands

LITTLE LAKE ROAD

COMPTCHE ROAD

BIG

RIVER

Little River

Mendocino

① 1

PACIFIC

OCEAN

BIG RIVER

0   1   2

MILES

The Mad River
(23 miles • CLASS II)

THE Mad springs out of the ridges of the southernmost end of the sprawling Six Rivers National Forest and snakes its way through the rugged isolation of the Eaton Roughs and into the gorges and canyons of the Humboldt National Forest on its 90-mile course to the Pacific just north of Arcata. Its drainage basin is narrow—closely flanked by those of the Van Duzen and South Fork of the Trinity—its tributaries are unimportant. The result is a short boating season and restricted access possibilities. But the scenery between the barren Eaton Roughs and the Iaqua Buttes on the river's unexplored middle section gives this part of the Mad fascinating exploring potential for expert boaters.

The river dries up in its upper reaches in the summer above Ruth Reservoir. Downstream from the earth-fill dam, the boating season seldom lasts beyond late spring, and sometimes less, depending on the winter rains. Wintertime itself offers some consistent flows in between high floods from heavy storms, but only for experienced boaters.

Ruth Dam to Highway 36 Bridge
(10 miles • CLASS II • Running Time 3 hours)
USGS 15 minute quadrangle map
"Pickett Peak"

• The river flows over a predominantly gravel bottom and is easily scouted by car along the Ruth Reservoir Road that parallels it from the Highway 36 cutoff to the base of the dam. Access to this beautiful rolling country is along Highway 36, either east out of Fortuna on U. S. 101 or west out of Red Bluff on Interstate 5. The Fortuna route is shorter, but the Red Bluff access is more scenic through the Trinity National Forest.

The put-in is just below the dam, and there is an equally convenient take-out at the Highway 36 bridge. Halfway down the run, on the right bank and where the river loops sharply

The Mad River's short boating season is marked
with boulderfields like this that make it a
demanding challenge for canoeists near Van Duzen
State Park. Its lower 12 mile run above its
junction with the Eel, however, offers much more
sedate water.

left, is the Mad River campground, a pleasant stopping point for a picnic or an overnight stay. While the water coming out of the bottom of the lake there is quite cold for swimming, it can provide a refreshing respite from the warm spring weather. The run can be stretched out considerably by linking up with the succeeding two segments.

Highway 36 Bridge to Lookout Road
(6 miles • CLASS II • Running Time 2 hours)
USGS 15 minute quadrangle maps
"Pickett Peak" and "Blocksburg"

• This is primarily a continuation of the conditions of the previous section, though the gradient is a bit steeper. It can be scouted in dry weather by the rather primitive dirt road along the east side, which follows the river from the bridge almost all the way to the take-out where Lookout Road crosses the river due east of Dinsmore. The Mad flows through an isolated canyon here, and in spring the three creeks on either side help beef up the flow a bit. The river is too small for big rafts, but is suitable for most other craft.

Lookout Road to Anderson Ford
(7 miles • CLASS II • Running Time 2½ hours)
USGS 15 minute quadrangle map
"Pilot Creek"

• This added stretch should be run only in dry weather because of the primitive dirt road access to the ford, about 4 miles north of the Dinsmore landing strip on Highway 36 just east of the town. Road conditions should be checked on in Dinsmore if there have been recent rains. In any case, boaters would be well advised to flag-mark the ford area when they drop their shuttle vehicle off here. This precaution is unnecessary if the car, trail bike, or whatever can be parked close enough to be seen from the river.

Downstream of Anderson Ford, the Mad needs further scouting—but only by well-trained teams. The next good access is 22 miles downstream, near the end of the gravel road 14 miles south of Maple Creek. The Six Rivers National Forest map is an excellent road access guide for the whole length of the Mad.

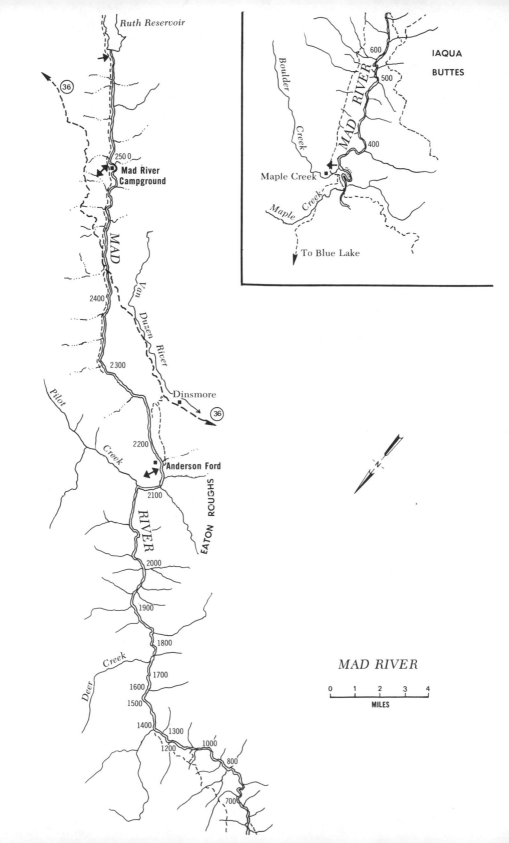

Ruth Reservoir

(36)

2500
Mad River
Campground

MAD

2400

Van Duzen River

2300

Pilot

Creek

Dinsmore

(36)

2200

Anderson Ford

2100

RIVER

EATON ROUGHS

2000

1900

1800

Deer Creek

1700

1600
1500

1400   1300

1200   1000

800

700

IAQUA

BUTTES

Boulder

Creek

600

500

MAD RIVER

400

Maple Creek

Maple   Creek

To Blue Lake

MAD RIVER

0   1   2   3   4
MILES

The Mattole River
(54 miles · CLASS I–III)

THE Mattole is one of the best coastal streams for boating, despite its rather abbreviated watershed and short length. But what it lacks in length, it more than makes up for with flow as a result of the yearly rainfall of 100 inches in the area. That certainly stretches out the boating season, although caution must be exercised to avoid the high flood crests after heavy rain storms. The rain that feeds the gravel stream bed also prompts luxuriant winter and springtime growth along the banks and high undulating hills that in spring are alive with a vibrant carpet of wildflowers.

Because the river is strictly rain-fed, its best running time is between early April and July. Still, early fall rains, before the weather turns excessively cold and while the autumnal color explosion is still on, often provide exquisite drifting along a predominantly gentle grade. Usually, however, unless the rainy season has exceeded 100 inches and stretched out into early April, the Mattole will have to be waded in many places later than early July.

Far off the beaten path—35 miles south of Eureka—the Mattole is reached by taking the Honeydew turnoff from U. S. 101, just north of Weott, and then a long, snaking ride up and over the ridge and down into Honeydew at streamside. You can also reach the river by another route, turning off 101 just north of Fortuna and heading south for Fernbridge and on to Petrolia on the lower Mattole. There is still another access further south, turning off 101 on the Redway off-ramp at Garberville and taking the Shelter Cove road as far as Briceland.

One of the larger and longer coastal streams, the
Mattole is flanked by greenery, most of it the
beginnings of second-growth forest. This passage
just downstream of Honeydew is representative of
Class I-II rating.

Shelter Cove Road Bridge to Ettersburg
(11 miles • CLASS II–IV • *Running Time 4½ hours)*
USGS 15 minute quadrangle map
"Garberville"

• The upper boating limit of the river is probably where the Shelter Cove Road crosses the Mattole between Whitehorn and Shelter Cove. This section, however, is more suited to kayaks and decked canoes because of the swift drops and rocky rapids. Just beyond the halfway mark are two chutes that should be portaged by all but experts. In between this point and the start, there are several challenging Class III rapids; but downstream of the last portage, the river begins to slow and takes on more of a Class II character. While this run starts out in splendid isolation among verdant, wooded hills, its lower stretches pass through sections which have been ravaged by the lumbermen.

Ettersburg to Honeydew
(18 miles • CLASS I–II • *Running Time 5½ hours)*
USGS 15 minute quadrangle map
"Point Delgada"

• Open canoes and small rafts can move onto the river here, launching from the same spot as the previous run's takeout—where the Honeydew Road crosses the river at Ettersberg. This ideal canoe water is mostly a placid stream with exciting riffles, a few sharp corners, and bouncy Class II dips for good measure. The flow is good enough and the gradient modest enough to permit a fairly easy one-day run, although it would be very difficult in that time during low-water periods.

At a more leisurely pace, taking time out for swimming and occasional visits to the pretty glades at streamside and their abundance of wild flowers, this run makes a perfect overnight trip. There is no road access between the launch and take-out, and the river meanders through several deep and pretty canyons. In the late fall and early winter, between heavy storm flows, the Mattole also has some of the coast's finer steelhead fishing.

As with all coastal streams, extreme care must be taken to avoid the tumultuous rainstorms and their heavy stream flows that cause rapid rises in water level. The rivers fall rather quickly,

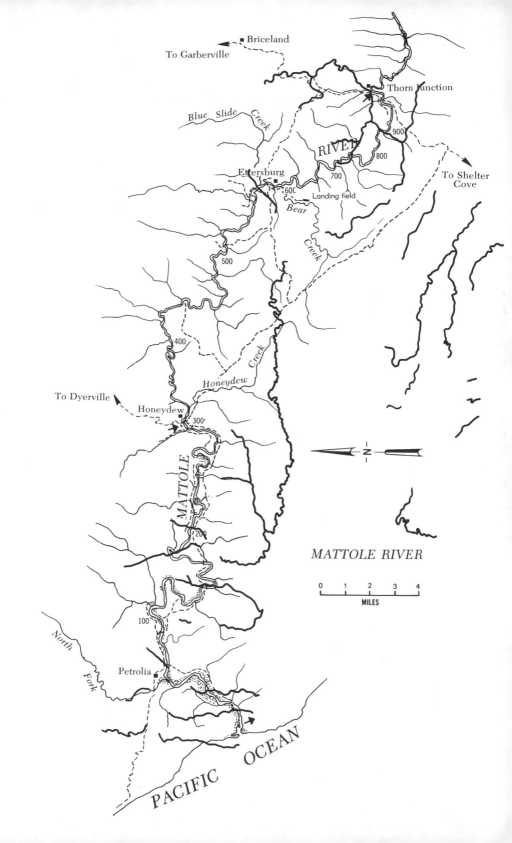

To Garberville ■ Briceland

Blue Slide Creek

Thorn Junction

900

800

Ettersburg

700

60C

Landing field

Bear

To Shelter Cove

500

Creek

400

Creek

Honeydew

To Dyerville

Honeydew

300

MATTOLE

200

MATTOLE RIVER

N

0 1 2 3 4
MILES

100

North Fork

Petrolia

PACIFIC OCEAN

too, and with the proper scouting of weather reports, the Mattole's season can be productive in the winter time. The lower runs especially would be safer at this time. A similar attention to weather reports and the precautions they signal must also be adhered to on the Sierra rivers when the spring melt sends every one of them speeding dangerously over their banks.

Just before the take-out at Honeydew, as the last canyon begins to widen out, there is the run's only Class III drop. The sound of rushing water gives an early warning. Take-out is best on the right and upstream side of the Honeydew bridge.

Honeydew to Petrolia
(*20 miles* • CLASS I–II • *Running Time 6 hours*)
USGS 15 minute quadrangle maps
"Scotia" and "Cape Mendocino"

• This is one of the river's more convenient runs. The gradient ranges from 12–20 feet per mile. The road parallels the river, crossing it at several places to afford excellent opportunity for car scouting as well as considerable flexibility in the length of the run. While not as isolated as the upper run, this section, with plenty of river bar campsites, is conducive to an overnight schedule. The final lap to the ocean and the beach just north of Punta Gorda lighthouse, an added 6 miles, would be particularly worthwhile for the rockhounds. Prized gemstone deposits glitter in the wash of the tide on the gravel bars at the Mattole's mouth. Of course, the tide will dictate whether you make the dash for the ocean, but if you do it, you must plan on either paddling all the way back to the Petrolia bridge or making a long carry-out to the lighthouse road, about 1½ miles.

Kayakers swirl through a looping but modest rapid along the Mattole River's lower stretches near Petrolia. Extended winter rainfall on its sizeable watershed prolong its prime boating season into early and, in wet years, midsummer.

The Navarro
(*22 miles* · CLASS I)

THE longest of the small coastal rivers, the Navarro has somehow managed to retain a little of its redwood-fringed beauty
despite the continuous logging action throughout its 50-mile watershed.

Greenwood Ridge Road to Dimmick State Park
(*22 miles* · CLASS I · *Running Time 7 hours*)
USGS 15 minute quadrangle maps
"Booneville" and "Navarro"

• The best access point for launching on this run is at the
Greenwood Ridge Road (County Road 132)—9 miles west of Booneville—where the road crosses the river on its way to Hendy
Woods State Park. The access involves a moderately steep carry
along a path on the south and downstream side of the bridge.

The course between here and the take-out at Paul Dimmick
State Park, where the North Fork joins the Navarro, is mostly
flat, moving water. The biggest problems are blowdowns and
brush piles along the narrow, twisting course of the stream. As
in the case of all coastal rivers, boaters must make sure to watch
the weather reports. Small rains are needed to get up a decent
head of water, but extensive winter rains can turn this peaceful
stream into a raging torrent.

Dimmick State Park has some ideal rough campsites for an
overnighter, although the river's best running time—November
to April, when not in flood stage—is hardly conducive to camping out. After the first rains in late fall, this run is a particularly
popular float trip for steelhead fishermen. The hole that the
North Fork has gouged out of the streambed is especially good
fishing.

The remaining 8 miles of water beyond Dimmick Park to the

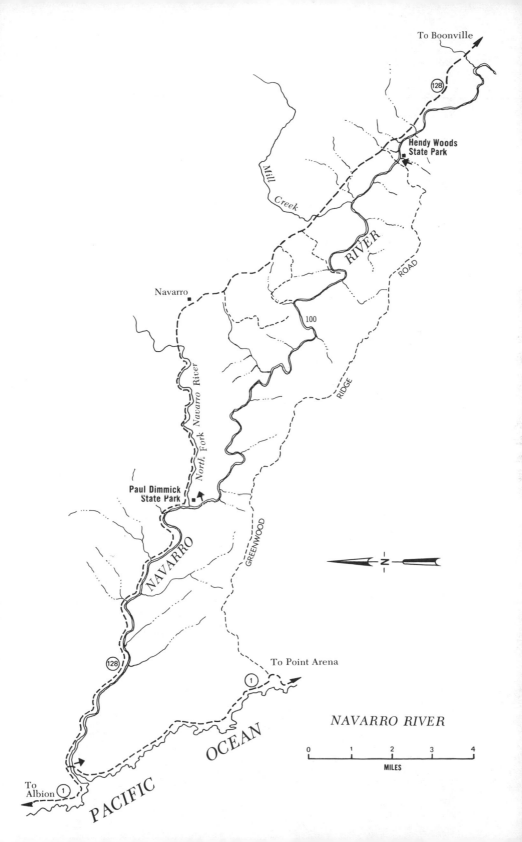

To Boonville

128

Hendy Woods
State Park

Mill Creek

RIVER

ROAD

Navarro

100

RIDGE

North Fork Navarro River

Paul Dimmick
State Park

NAVARRO

GREENWOOD

N

To Point Arena

128

1

NAVARRO RIVER

PACIFIC

OCEAN

To
Albion 1

| 0 | 1 | 2 | 3 | 4 |

MILES

Highway 1 bridge are ideal for beginners and those who just like to drift through flat, easy water. Snags and an occasional brush pile are the only obstacles. Those who prefer the rich bird life of tidal reaches can continue the 2 miles to the ocean as the river stretches through a rich marshland abounding with egrets, herons, and a variety of other birds. There is no road access, however, and you will have to paddle back upstream to the bridge—actually, not much of a task in this almost-still water.

The scenic and popular Navarro River is 22 miles of slow-moving water surrounded by tall pines and a few choice specimens of virgin growth redwood in Dimmick State Park. It holds equal allure to all boaters but its boating season is quite short, seldom beyond late May.

The Noyo River
(*12 miles* • CLASS I–II)

SIFTING into the blue Pacific at Fort Bragg, the Noyo was more popular with hardy wintertime canoeists when the Northwestern Pacific Railroad's famed Skunk line was still carrying passengers. Boaters could be dropped off by the train at any of a dozen spots. Now that the line has been discontinued for passenger use, however, access is more of a problem.

Information and permission to use the private logging roads for upriver access should be sought from the Redwood Industry Recreation Association in Fort Bragg. Most of the logging roads are open to boaters and anglers only on the weekend and the permitted use times are clearly posted. If there is any question, check with the owners—first of all, because it is private property, and, secondly, because the logging operation can be hazardous to an unexpected intruder.

Fort Bragg to Noyo Harbor
(*12 miles* • CLASS I–II • *Running Time 4 hours*)
USGS 15 minute quadrangle maps
"Comptche" and "Fort Bragg"

• During weekends, a private logging road is open for river access just north of the A&W Root Beer stand on the east side of Highway 1 in Fort Bragg, half a mile north of the Noyo River bridge. It is 6 miles along this logging road to the first bridge. The North Fork comes into the Noyo at this point. Boaters can either launch here for a fairly short run or take the lefthand road after crossing the bridge and continue up the canyon another 4 miles to a low wooden bridge.

There are some short drops and exciting chutes and glides on this upper section of the Noyo as it twists down through the canyon. There is nothing dangerous, however; the most common problems on this, and other coastal streams, are deadfalls, blowdowns, and brush. Still, the velvet-like carpet of green and the towering redwoods that flank the river make the tour more than worthwhile. Steelhead fishing is also quite good in these rivers after the fall rains begin.

Boaters should be prepared to make a few short portages around deadfalls, and even a few when the river shallows up considerably; but they will all be short and not very demanding. The lower 7 miles of the river, particularly, are quite flat, but still very pretty and absolutely isolated from civilization.

The take-out access is near a small boat crane in the Noyo Harbor, connected on the north side of the river by Harbor Road. Similar take-out access is also available on the south side, reached from Highway 1 by turning off on Highway 20 a short distance from the river.

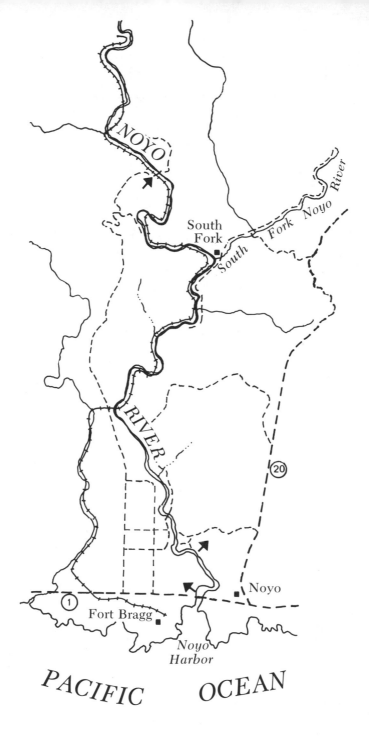

NOYO

South
Fork

South Fork Noyo River

RIVER

(20)

(1)

Noyo

Fort Bragg

Noyo
Harbor

PACIFIC   OCEAN

NOYO RIVER

0   1   2

MILES

The Russian River
(*60 miles* • CLASS I–II)

AN ideal stretch of 60 miles from the Lake Mendocino Dam near Ukiah to its scenic delta at Jenner-by-the-Sea, the Russian is a river of many moods. Heavy winter rains turn it into a rampaging monster almost annually, but in between floods it may be the most ideal boating water in the state, offering perfect conditions for beginning and experienced boaters alike.

Accessibility is one of the greatest assets of the river. Its entire length is flanked by good roads; U. S. 101 parallels its headwaters from near the Lake Mendocino dam to Healdsburg, and from there to Guerneville, a paved road connects to State Route 116, which goes all the way to the coast.

Whatever arguments can be made against damming up free-flowing rivers—and they are many and profound in most cases—the control of the Russian keeps it from thinning down too low for passage in the later summer and fall. Even the minimum flow makes for ideal canoeing as late as December, depending upon the weather, of course. There are also periods of high water in January and February when the crispness and isolation add another dimension to this busy stretch. While the high water runs a swifter course, it also flattens out the riffles and many of the short, tricky maneuvers they demand. Except at flood stage, the river is almost always safe.

Cloverdale to Alexander Valley Bridge
(*15 miles* • CLASS I–II • *Running Time 5 hours*)
USGS 15 minute quadrangle maps
"Hopland," "Kelseyville," and *"Healdsburg"*

• Most of the water above Cloverdale is suited to kayaks or small canoes. Even then, there are some rocky stretches where wading is compulsory. But from the Cloverdale bridge on U.S. 101 down, canoeing is ideal almost the year around. The run

The popularity of the Russian River is unequalled,
both because of the availability of rental boats and
the river's small but exciting nature.

from Cloverdale to Jenner is a relatively easy five-day trip. Speed demons could make the run in about half the time, of course, but this schedule permits plenty of leisure time for swimming and early camps along the way. The stretch can also easily be divided into a series of ideal one-day runs. The Trowbridge Russian River Canoe Rentals at Healdsburg can supply information on camping grounds and river conditions, and on boats as well. The company also offers shuttle service back to customer's car if there is only one car in the party.

Boaters can also launch from the upstream side of Asti bridge. This is east of the Italian Swiss Colony winery and is reached by turning east onto a river road that is half a mile south of the winery off-ramp from the freeway. The ideal take-out for an easy 5-hour run from Asti would be the Alexander Valley bridge, easily accessible for a shuttle car on Highway 21 from Healdsburg. The Asti–Alexander Valley stretch is a pleasant mixture of small riffles, moderate rapids, and deep, placid pools. The river is not large enough to be much of a threat. No boater has drowned in the estimated one million trips down the river in the past 25 years. The most consistent difficulty is lack of elbow room in clearing the chutes. The tight quarters put a premium on pulling out of currents at the base of a run in order to avoid being swept into the underbrush that lines both banks.

In springtime, high water flattens out most of the rapids, but the result is still acceptable. Drifters can make good time with only occasional strokes for steering, and there are few pleasures to match the peacefulness of drifting quietly, effortlessly, downstream, drinking in every foot of scenery along the way.

Alexander Valley Bridge to Healdsburg
(*14 miles* • CLASS I • *Running Time 4½ hours*)
USGS 15 minute quadrangle map
"Healdsburg"

• The next 15 miles of river, from Alexander Valley to Healdsburg Memorial Beach, offers the most exciting combination of small, fun rapids, and quiet pools on the river. The stream is also canopied with an umbrella of greenery that makes civilization seem a long way off. Again, the challenges are to avoid being spun around in the back-eddies of the bigger runs or being

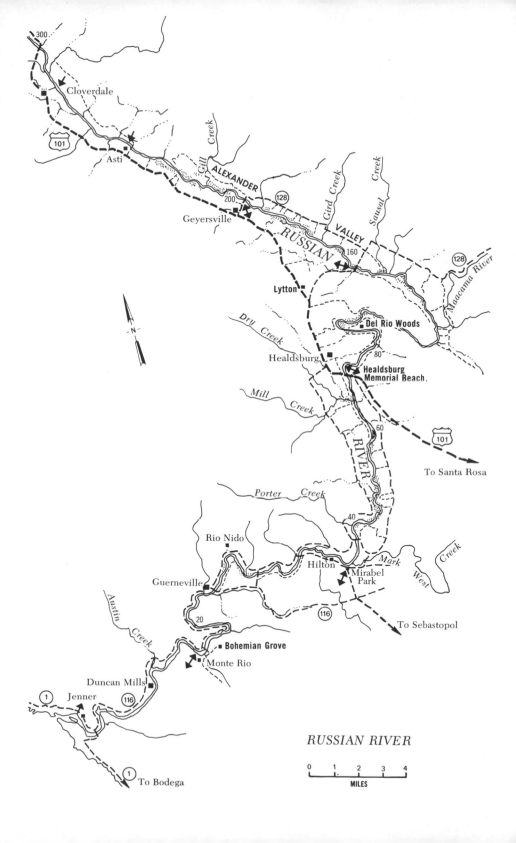

RUSSIAN RIVER

0 1 2 3 4
MILES

swept by the current into brush and logs. Although the river modifies its channel from year to year, the safest passage, at least the deepest water, can usually be charted by sticking closest to the side with the steepest banks.

About two hours below the Alexander Valley bridge is the most demanding turn on the whole river. A large sugarloaf boulder juts up out of the landscape to mark the place. Here, the river piles headlong into the face of the rock and then careens sharply to the right. The approach is narrow, but greenhorns and the more sedate boaters can easily beach on the left-bank gravel bar above this spot. Those who wish to proceed should stay to the left fork in front of the rock, remaining in the center of the slick and then cutting sharply to the right out of the current to avoid the rock. From there it is merely a matter of riding the exciting crest of some fair-sized rollers into the flat water below. The right-hand fork is cramped between clumps of willows but much slower and safer. As always, it is better to beach above the rapids, then walk down and scout out your own pathway. This bit of preventive caution should be the first commandment in all river runs.

Beyond this mild obstruction, the most serious challenge on the Russian is making your way through channels in the sometimes ankle-deep bars. In early spring, when the water is high and before the floodgates go into action, shallow water is no problem. In addition, the current is swift enough to almost obviate the need for anything but directional stroking. But from late spring until the day after Labor Day, when the temporary dams at Healdsburg and Del Rio Woods are put in, these lower stretches of the Russian offer tough still-water canoeing at the end of the trip, sometimes against brisk upriver winds that put a premium on muscles and teamwork. Another complication is that power boats buzz these stretches, often making it quite apparent that canoes are not entirely welcome on these waters.

Healdsburg to Jenner-by-the-Sea
(31 miles • CLASS I • Running Time 10 hours)
USGS 15 minute quadrangle maps
"Healdsburg," "Sebastopol," and "Duncan Mills"

• Below the Healdsburg bridge over 101, the river returns to a bustling little string of small riffles, modest glides, and quiet pools as it meanders through the acres of vineyards and orchards that dot the fertile valley. In this section of the river, there are many possibilities for short one-day and two-day jaunts. The first 5-hour lap is from the bridge down to either Mirabel Park beach, where camping is permitted at a modest fee, or to Hilton, just a mile or two further on. Then, on the following day, the beautiful redwoods flank the river as it cuts through the coastal range, skirting the Korbel winery and vineyards and passing Guerneville and the world-renowned Bohemian Grove to Monte Rio beach. From Monte Rio, it is just another 2 miles through the flattened delta leading to Jenner-by-the-Sea, with its quaint and rustic scenery and its intriguing patchwork of bird and marine life and dazzling land and sea scapes.

The Russian slows its pace noticeably through this stretch, and there is more population along its shores—especially once you clear Guerneville, where summer cabins begin popping up along the banks like so many mushrooms. But the redwoods, the mountains, and the tangy salt air of the ocean are strongly offsetting factors to these signs of civilization. Access and take-out points are naturally plentiful all along this stretch.

To sum up, then, the Russian is really the "best bet" for the beginner. First of all, there is the Trowbridge Canoe Rentals. It is one of the biggest such agencies in the world and it has an astounding safety record. The beginner can take his halting first strokes without having to make a major investment. Further, the Russian is the kind of river in which the beginner can get his feet (and more) wet without any harrowing mishaps. Fast enough to be fun, the river is nevertheless neither wide enough nor wild enough to be a threat. Beginners can acquire a sound style and education in most of the fast-water maneuvers needed for bigger water in less than a full season on this stream. In fact, with the proper beginning in a Red Cross, American Canoe Association, or Sierra Club training and canoe-safety course, it would only take a run or two on the Russian to be ready to graduate to bigger, tougher water.

Afterword

This volume was not merely designed to be a "how-to" guide. I have endeavored to introduce you to some of the wondrous resources of California's river system. And I hope that I have also made you aware of how precious this resource is and how easily it may be sapped by the senseless and uncaring. Our family prays that you too will feel and respond to the vibrant reawakening that the remaining rivers and their life systems touched off in us. And we hope then that you will join us in guarding against the misuse that has already spoiled and shrunk so much of the dimensions and beauty of the California wild rivers. We hope that you will dedicate yourselves to a gift that will keep on giving forever—leaving these magical sanctuaries unspoiled and preserved for your children and their children and others to come.

Index

The author, a native of Canada, first cut his teeth on a paddle on the pristine waters of Waterton Lakes National Park in his home province of Alberta. A career journalist, he was Outdoors Editor for one of Canada's largest newspapers and now is Environmental Writer for the San Jose Mercury-News.

A founder and two-time president of the California Academy of Environmental Newswriters, the 38-year-old writer in 1970 was named California's outstanding conservation writer by the California Wildlife Federation.

He has served as consultant to the Governor's Conference on California's Changing Environment and been active in the campaign for Sen. Peter Behr's Wild and Scenic Rivers Bill.

He has attended and participated in national and international conferences on the environment, been singled out in two studies of environmental reporting as the state's leading environmental journalist, and has lectured on the subject at Stanford University and the University of Texas.

His boating exploits have taken him, his wife Glenda and their three children down most of California's premier canoeing water. Down the Wild Rivers